My Best Friends Speak in Whinnies

My Best Friends
Speak in Whinnies

By Rubye Mae Griffith

SOUTH BRUNSWICK AND NEW YORK:
A. S. BARNES AND COMPANY
LONDON: THOMAS YOSELOFF LTD

A. S. Barnes and Co., Inc.

Cranbury, New Jersey 08512

Thomas Yoseloff Ltd

18 Charing Cross Road

London, W.C. 2, England

6672

Printed in the United States of America

Contents

My Best Friends Speak in Whinnies

Prologue

The Trap — And the Escape!

Once I was trapped in a Squirrel Cage!

It was a comfortable, well-furnished Squirrel Cage, on Madison Avenue, in Word City.

I went round and round inside my Squirrel Cage and spent all my time writing television commercials.

After I wrote them, I rewrote them.

Then I wrote rewrites of the rewrites.

This kept me busy. So busy that I felt quite contented inside my Squirrel Cage.

The keepers of my Squirrel Cage fostered this illusion. They were always pleasant, approving, and generous to a fault.

They literally snowed me with lettuce.

As time went by these friendly keepers hung ever more impressive titles on the door of my Squirrel Cage. And they gave me more and more lettuce.

Sometimes I'd slip away for a few hours to a little pad that I reached by means of an underground tunnel called "The Shuttle."

Here I laughed and played with my fellow-squirrels.

9

When I wasn't laughing or playing I spent my time counting my lettuce.

But sometimes I'd look off in the distance, across the bright, shiny ribbon of the Hudson River, to the pungently fragrant meadows of Jersey and I'd wonder: "What is life like outside my Squirrel Cage?"

There didn't seem to be any way of finding out.

It seemed frightening to think about breaking out of the Squirrel Cage. I'd have to go out there in the big, cruel world and leave behind all my lettuce!

Then one day my decision was made for me!

The trap opened and I escaped from my cage.

It all came about in the most remarkable way.

I was taking a little exercise (which you have to do when you live in a Squirrel Cage, if you want to keep fit—productive is the way my keepers would phrase it) and I met a Horse Lover!

In Central Park.

And he married me!

That's how I escaped.

I escaped from my well-furnished, lettuce-lined Squirrel Cage on Madison Avenue and I fled, with my Horse Lover, to the rough, rugged reaches of "The Bar None," a Horse Ranch in Southern California.

There, as the wife of my Horse Lover, I have become what is known as a Professional Pooper-Scooper, which means that I follow the horses. Not at the track. With a shovel.

I also act as midwife in my Horse Lover's Mare-ternity Ward. (I assisted at the delivery of seventeen colts one year.)

I have discovered what it is like to live with polygamists, endomorphs, psychopaths, and bums.

But all that is What Followed After—after my escape from the Squirrel Cage. . . .

What Followed After

1

Big Mama —
A Girl Mixed Up About Sex

No Bonanza-like spread is the Bar None; it is just a pocket size, wisp of a ranch, encircled by gaunt, sallow mountains and capped by the dome of the sky.

Within this sun-drenched and sage-scented world, so different from the world of Word City, the horses are a privileged class. Their needs come first. And they should. The horses are the breadwinners of the ranch. They are petted and pampered, and when we're lucky the horses are sold.

I should be happy when this happens, but I'm not. Because horses have become my best friends.

My husband Frank takes a different view of horses.

"Horses are a commodity," he says. "Merchandise to be marketed, the same as hay, or peanuts or words."

But in spite of these seemingly brash declarations, whenever Frank goes to a horse auction he seldom buys a horse that is marketable. Instead he buys one he feels sorry for. A nag in pitiful condition that he thinks he should rescue before it turns into dog food.

That's how he came to buy Big Mama.

My first glance at Big Mama convinced me that she must be a reincarnation of Roxinante, Don Quixote's sorry equine companion.

A liver-colored chestnut with a mane and tail once flaxen now turned drably puce, Big Mama stood sixteen three at the withers and had a rib cage the size of a mastodon's. You could hang your hat on her hip bones and sink a fist in her flank.

Apparently Big Mama had come to grips with several brawnier horses in transit, because every inch of her poor bony body was covered with bruises and toothmarks.

"She'll look different when she fattens up and you'll see she paces," said Frank. He could tell by my expression that I was wondering how anyone could buy such a wreck.

In view of his enthusiasm I took a better look at her.

A pacer. That meant she had probably raced in harness. A mare just like her might have been the mother of the immortal Dan Patch! Pacers are known to be gangly and raw-boned. But how could Frank see all these Hidden Potentials where I saw only a broken-down plug?

"The eye sees what the world presents to it; the heart beholds what God hath wrought." It was a favorite saying of mine. But it was Frank who had demonstrated it.

Suddenly grateful that I had married a man who judges not by the appearance, but by righteous judgment, I threw my arms around Frank and bussed him heartily.

"What are you trying to do, make me swallow my pipe? What was that for?" he growled.

"For being you. Eighteen months and a hundred bales of hay from now I'm sure this dainty critter will make a beautiful show horse! I move we call her Big Mama!"

And that's how Big Mama was named.

Big Mama proved to have the disposition of an angel, the appetite of a grist mill.

Possibly this was because she had always been used as a brood mare and had eaten for two for so long that she had to keep up the good work. From the distention of her milk glands and the circumference of her girth it was obvious that she must have been producing offspring most of her life.

Like many who have suffered great deprivation, Big Mama found it difficult to believe the depression was over. If left to her own devices, she would consume a hundred-and-eighty-pound bale of hay every day. Apparently Big Mama was trying to reassure herself that for the present, at least, she didn't have to go hungry. But when she had finally stowed away such vast quantities of hay that her hunger was partially assuaged, she would occasionally stop eating long enough to let me groom her.

Before long Big Mama began to take an interest in her appearance and actually looked forward to her daily beauty ritual.

We bleached her mane and tail to their original flaxen hue and carefully combed out the snarls. We applied vaseline to all her bruises and scars so that her hair grew back over the blemishes. We curried her for hours at a time, painstakingly polishing her by hand, and after a few weeks of this constant attention her ego-image began to improve.

I don't mean to imply that she became spirited.

But she lifted her head off the ground and now and then emitted a shrill whinny.

When she was at last sufficiently rested to be put under saddle, Frank let me ride Big Mama. And it was true! She had one gentle, unchanging gait—an easy-going pace. You didn't have to touch her mouth or apply any aids. She went into her pace and stayed in it. An automatic horse.

At last we had a horse I could ride!

Yes, I have a sinful secret.

Though married to a horse lover I am deathly afraid of horses. And they know it.

If I reach out to pat a horse it lays its ears back and curls it lips at me—in a sneer.

If I attempt to put my foot in the stirrup it will back away, leaving me to hang in mid-air.

If I manage to haul myself into the saddle the horse rolls its eyes and looks me over appraisingly, then turns its head away in disgust.

Frank has tried, ever since our initial encounter in Central Park, to make a rider out of me. But he's about given up. Horses aren't as dumb as they look. They know they can take advantage of me. And they do.

The result is exasperation for Frank; humiliation for me.

But Big Mama was a horse I could trust, so I claimed her for my own. And since no customer appeared to contest my claim, she remained MY HORSE.

I knew the sight of money dangled enticingly within sight of my horse lover would immediately change all this, but until such time as a bid was made for her, I intended to enjoy Big Mama.

Big Mama began to put on weight. Her angular corners rounded into feminine curves and I dreamed my private day-dreams about her. I couldn't keep my dreams to myself very long and found myself blurting them out to Frank.

"Honey." This is always a good beginning. "Is there any chance that Big Mama could be bred?"

"At her age!" Frank was horrified.

"Look what happened to Elizabeth in the Bible."

"Well, I *have* known mares to produce fine foals long after they were twenty."

That did it. Frank agreed to a vet check. If the vet said Big Mama was capable of having a foal safely, we would breed her.

I watched at a ladylike distance as Frank assisted the vet in making the examination.

At its conclusion they moved toward me and their expressions were so peculiar I didn't know what to think. Was Big Mama long past her colt-bearing years? Was there something wrong with her?

They burst out laughing at my questions.

The examination had revealed that Big Mama was already in foal.

Whether it would be the offspring of a dray horse, a jackass or a donkey we had no way of knowing. For since she had been purchased at auction it was possible that she had been bred, unintentionally, in transit or by some bull-headed stud at the auction yards. Time alone would reveal the answer.

Of all the mares at the Bar None I loved Big Mama most.

Perhaps because I felt so sorry for her. She'd obviously led a hard life, had suffered greatly at the hands of man, and now was destined to bear a foal in her sunset years. I went to great lengths to encourage a friendship with her.

In fact, during the latter weeks of her pregnancy, I spent most of my spare time with her. I would sit close to her head in the summer evenings and listen as she chomped her hay, remaining at her side until darkness enfolded us. And when Frank completed the last round of lock-up chores, he would join us.

I studied her sad, equine face till I knew it as the face of a friend. Her near eye had a peculiar marble-like mottling around the eyeball which I recall in all its intricate veinings. Her nose had a spill of white against the blue-grey muzzle that rippled and rolled as she wound in her hay. Her teeth were sloping, elongated, stained, bespeaking a venerable age. Her hoofs were square and ragged, sad witnesses to callous neglect. Her belly had stretched to gigantic proportions and her bag, unable to accommodate the super-abundance of milk she produced, overflowed at each step.

Usually mares have their foals within forty-eight hours after the milk begins to spurt this way, but Big Mama had been sloshing milk for two or three days, wthout any further developments.

Since we had no record of a breeding date on which to approximate her date of confinement, we could only watch and wonder. When a foal is really imminent the mare usually goes off her feed but Big Mama continued to chomp her hay with customary avidity.

As I sat beside her in the back corral I wondered what she was thinking. She had a sad-eyed gaze that always seemed to rest on infinity. It was completely inscrutable . . .

Is she recalling the days of her youth when she flashed around the harness track—winning honors, acclaim, and possibly a brilliant collection of trophies, long since forgotten and covered with dust?

I take my eyes off the placid, imperturbable profile to stare at the mountains.

Pale drifts of fog veil their sloping brown shoulders.

The canyon breeze smacks of sea saltiness.

Granville and Gloria, our devoted guinea fowl, pad slowly past, whispering throaty endearments to one another, heading for their roost. They are followed by the chickens who also move with end-of-day indolence.

Westward the green-blue sky is etched with a silver tracery of jet trailings. The planes themselves are lost to view, but the shifting, feathered patterns linger, troubled by wind currents. Slowly they rearrange themselves in spectacular linear abstracts, lambent and wide as the world.

My eyes return to Big Mama. She has moved away.

I spring erect, my heart pounding.

"Frank! Hurry!"

He recognizes panic; a "drop everything" cry.

As he reaches my side I point a shaking finger toward Big Mama and now the time for shouting is over and I whisper softly:

"Big Mama is having her foal!"

As might be expected in a matriarch of Big Mama's years and fecundity, the period of accouchement was brief.

Big Mama brought forth her foal with the placidity of a peon.

Still winding in hay, which she consumed until the last possible moment, Big Mama lay down, stretched out on her side, and as the water bag broke, before our very eyes she produced a giant of a colt.

First came the neat little forehoofs, poking out through the tough, parachute silk of the clear white sac that foals float in during the more than eleven months of their gestation.

The forehoofs were followed by a pink nose and massive head. The foal was arriving in proper sequence!

The shoulders emerged, followed by a slick shining body and long, long hind legs.

No matter how many foals we have at the Bar None, we never relax till we're absolutely certain mother and child are out of danger. A mare in good condition should have her foal quickly and easily, without strain or discomfort. Big Mama was having a normal delivery. But we'd never seen such a large foal!

There was just enough daylight left for us to make out that she'd had a boy; deep chestnut in color, with a sorrel mane and tail. And apparently he had no reason to be ashamed of his paternal ancestor. For in spite of his great size he had a nicely cast head and showed good conformation.

After the foal was clear Big Mama lay stretched out for a few minutes, gathering strength. But her son was impatient to be on his feet and began inching away from her. His chest, his girth, his neck, gave the impression that he was at least two months old.

Before Big Mama could get to her feet, he stood up. This broke the umbilical cord in the way that nature intended and he was free. Immediately he staggered around on his long, gangly legs, and though unsteady and wobbly, he at least remained standing.

In a few minutes Big Mama struggled to her feet and gave a

motherly nicker. Her colt responded with a whinny that startled us—it was so lusty. Not at all the sort of sound you'd expect to emerge from a newborn infant!

I reached out and touched him. His coat was still damp from amniotic fluid, but soft and silky. The wonder, the warmth, and the beauty of him—his skittery gangliness and perfect little horsiness—filled me with awe.

I find that I feel the same reverent awesomeness each time a new foal arrives at the Bar None.

Big Mama, too, seemed to experience great stirrings of feeling. She whinnied constantly, deep-throated velvety gurglings that were obviously intended to inspire her offspring with courage. She sniffed at him; nuzzled him; ran a rough pink tongue against the grain of his coat. The mares are always fiercely protective right after foaling and Big Mama ran true to form.

"We must get them in the stable," said Frank, and together we pushed Big Mama, pulled the colt; then pulled the colt and pushed Big Mama till finally she lumbered into the stall and Frank lifted the colt bodily and set him down beside her.

Frank gave Big Mama a warm bran mash and instantly she forgot her foal completely and devoured the mash in huge mouthfuls.

All those tender gurglings hadn't been for her colt after all; they were simply an expression of hunger!

When we first started raising horses at the Bar None, I would always give the deepest thought to the selection of a proper name for each new young 'un. Names had to be chosen with proper regard for family blood lines and must reflect delicate nuances of character, disposition, or performance potential. This conscientiousness lessened as more and more mares begat more and more foals.

By the time Big Mama had her colt I was ready to agree with Frank that Dan Patch would make an excellent name for him.

"Dan Patch was just about the greatest pacer of all time. Do you think our Dan will break his record some day?" I asked.

Frank gave me a look which reminded me that Big Mama was only a grade mare and Dan was a love child, so he could never be entered in a racing competition with blooded horses, because he could never be registered.

This didn't dampen Dan's spirit.

He was awkward as most oversize youngsters are. But he had a gentle eye and an appealing manner that quickly endeared him to all of us.

Big Mama gave enough milk for three colts and Dan had the appetite of three so he grew rapidly. In fact, at four weeks he looked like a colt of six months.

We don't keep a stud at the Bar None so whenever our mares come in season we send them away to be bred.

When it came time for Big Mama to go on her romantic pilgrimage, we bundled her off with Dan at her side, confident that she would take the stud immediately, remain at the stud farm three weeks so that she could be checked out as "settled"; then we would trailer her home.

But at the end of three weeks the owner of the stud farm called to say that Big Mama had turned out to be the strangest mare he'd ever tried to breed—and this after twenty years of breeding mares.

"Usually we breed a mare three or four times and that's it," Mr. Moss explained to Frank, his voice shaky with amazement. "If they're 'in' they take the stud okay; after that they give him a good swift kick if he comes messing 'round. But your mare, Big Mama . . . " words failed him.

He tried again.

"Your mare, Big Mama, took the stud eighteen times so far. and kept eating her hay all the time. In plain horse language, Mr. Griffith, I think your Big Mama's a . . . "

Frank coughed loudly, knowing I was listening on the extenson phone. "Send her on home," he told Mr. Moss. "She's probably too old to breed."

But Big Mama fooled him.

The vet check reported her "settled."

We don't know whether it was the first or the eighteenth try that did it, but Big Mama was once more in foal.

Because of her advanced years, her prodigious appetite and her generally doleful disposition, Big Mama always got more than her share of attention. The other mares—who were young, quick-tempered, and jealous—took exception to this favoritism and would gang up on Big Mama any time she was turned out to pasture. They managed to get her cornered, then they let her have it. Hoofs would fly, teeth snap and we'd find Big Mama covered with bruises and battle scars. I'd rescue her, tie her to the hitching rail, and paint her many wounds with gentian violet. One day I left her tied this way, went to attend to some other chores, and forgot her. When I thought of her again she was nowhere in sight.

Eventually I tracked her to the granary.

She'd eaten almost a sack of grain, was standing bleary eyed and puffing, her stomach distended—obviously a victim of colic. Colic, a distressing condition caused by an intestinal kink, causes great suffering in horses; it can sometimes prove fatal and is the bugaboo of every horse owner. When a horse has the colic it paws the ground, switches its tail, breaks out in a sweat, and will eventually lie down to roll in agony. Once down, it is usually impossible to get the stricken animal to its feet and many a fine horse is lost this way. When we spot colic symptoms we call the vet immediately and get ready for a long, painful vigil. The horse must be kept on its feet and walking continuously until it has a normal bowel movement.

For some reason the horses at the Bar None always seem to develop colic late Sunday evening when the vets are happily bedded down and the only reply to your cry for help is the sugared voice of their answering service. Or, if colic doesn't turn up at the end of a long, hard week end, it waits until the weather is threatening.

The day Big Mama gorged herself on grain and wound up pawing the ground and biting at her flank, gigantic white clouds were piled high on the horizon. And just as Big Mama groaned mightily and got ready to lie down, a tortured wind roared through the tops of the eucalyptus trees, rattling the tarps that anchor our hay stacks; overturning swings and lawn furniture, whipping the poor denuded elms to a frenzy.

Only the week before the Santa Anas had blown, hot and dry from the desert. Electricity crackled in the horses' tails. Night temperatures seldom dropped below seventy. Although it was mid-November, summer lingered on as it often does in Southern California.

But now, with the shift in wind, summer had ended. In twenty minutes the temperature dropped to below forty.

Huge drops of rain, scudding before the wind, felt icy cold as they hit my skin. And where they splashed in the pasture each raised a puff ball of dust.

As the rain increased, settling the dust, the acrid smell of iron rose from the parched ground. It is the smell that always goes with our first rain and is caused by the heavy mineral content of our soil.

Now the rain swept over the mountains in a silver sheet and the sharp iron smell was replaced by the musk-laden odor of wet manure.

"Get the rain things and hurry!" Frank shouted above the wind's wail as he dragged Big Mama toward the tack room. "We'll take turns walking her."

I ran to the house and searched frantically for slickers, ponchos, anything that would hold off the water. But rain things, during the dry season in California, are as neglected as a mother-in-law on a wedding trip. I stood on my head, clawing through chests, boxes, and closets. Finally I unearthed two raincoats, one hat, and two pairs of boots. One raincoat was shredded from dry rot. (It's a long time between drinks for thirsty rubber in these parts—sometimes as long as ten months.)

I ran with the good raincoat to Frank who had just finished saddling up his horse, Sir James. Under the stress of circumstances I forgot everything Frank had taught me about the safe way to approach a horse when you're carrying an unidentified flying object.

Torents of rain poured from eaves and drain spouts. The ranch yard was a slick sea of 'dobe. In the center of the morass Frank was lifting a foot to the stirrup when I arrived with rain coat flapping. Instantly his horse shied and dumped him in a thick soup of mud.

The air turned blue with expletives as Frank struggled to his feet—still hanging onto the reins, good horseman that he is!

I cringed beneath the gushing rain spout, wishing with all my heart that I had never left my cozy squirrel cage to become a rancher's wife.

But not for long.

Sir James, now thoroughly spooked, refused to allow Frank to mount him. It was the crackle of the raincoat that bugged him. So Frank had to remove the raincoat and ride with water streaming off his hat, down his jacket and into his boots.

In spite of my really inexcusable *faux pas,* I had to be pressed into service. Every fifteen minutes one of us would go inside and dry out while the other took over leading Big Mama. Through this system of relays we hoped to last longer. When it came my turn to mount the lead horse, Sir James, he refused to stand at the mounting block and I couldn't get on him. So I lead Big Mama on foot.

I wore a raincoat that came to my heels, hip boots and gloves and a "Uneeda Biscuit Boy" hat, with a back flap reminiscent of the Foreign Legion. Thus protected from the rain, I couldn't see how I could possibly mind a measly fifteen minutes of exercise. But as I slipped and slid in the 'dobe, with Big Mama slipping and sliding at my heels, the fifteen minutes seemed endless. How happy I was to see Frank reappear to do his stint!

We had started the wood fire in the kitchen and it was sheer bliss to snuggle up to it, so close that it sizzled my britches.

We maintained our vigil, firing the stove when on house duty, plodding silently through the splashing mud and sloshing rain when it came time to switch.

As I walked beside Big Mama I would stop every so often to press my ear to her flank. Frank told me that if I heard Niagara-like roarings or rumblings, it would be a sign that her intestines were functioning once more and the crisis might be over. But all remained silent within the cavern of her mighty belly.

Some time around 10 P.M. we heard a car buck its way down the rutted lane, windshield wipers flapping. Out jumped the vet, smiling and cheerful, in a yellow slicker. He'd delivered two foals that night, sewed up a wire cut, and was headed for a neighboring ranch where a Hereford had just produced twins.

He gave Big Mama a shot and a drenching (guaranteed to physic her) and advised us to: "Keep her moving, keep her moving, no matter what!"

We watched the tail lights of his wagon disappear in the dripping black void that ringed the stable lights, and immediately returned to our posts.

It was Frank's turn to replenish the coffee pot; mine to make the rounds with Big Mama.

Slip, slop, slip. Slosh, splash, slosh.

My legs ached clear to my shoulders. Only by the most determined exertion of will was I able to lift one mud-encased boot and place it ahead of the other.

The rain had increased to a steady downpour, but mercifully the wind had lessened. Big Mama, who was just as bone weary as I, had to be pushed, prodded, cajoled, coaxed, threatened, yanked, wheedled, and shoved; and then she moved at a snail's pace. Every few inches she would try to lie down and I would crack my whip at her, but I cracked it on the wet ground; I simply could not bring myself to hit her with it.

At 1 A.M., making my rounds again, I noted that the rain had stopped and the wind, whipping down from icier heights, knifed through the dampness of my jacket and ran its cold fingers down my neck. Through the black, scudding clouds the moon raced on to infinity, splattering the trees with a silvered radiance.

The lights in the stable area kept the other horses awake and they thrust their heads out of their stalls and whinnied inquisitively as Big Mama and I thwomped by. I could imagine their comments as we shuffled past them.

"What's the matter, old girl? Been hogging it again?"

"Don't tell me you're that way again—at your age!"

I handed the reins over to Frank as he mounted Sir James for the umpeenth time and scurried back to the warmth of the wood stove.

Since I am considered a city slicker I make it a point never to complain about my ranch duties. But I had the feeling I was about to spoil my record. It would be so nice to lie down and doze off, if only for a few minutes. It wouldn't matter much where. I could even imagine curling up in the middle of a nice, juicy mud puddle.

I brewed a fresh pot of coffee and just as I was about to sample it, I heard a knock at the door, and it opened.

Our neighbor, Joan Benson, ducked into the kitchen. She wore a chic evening dress and stole and held a newspaper over her head. I hadn't seen a newspaper used for an umbrella since I left my Squirrel Cage and the scurrying commuters of Grand Central Station.

"Just getting home from a night of fun and frolic," said Joan. "And I saw your stable lights. I figured it must be colic, but never dreamed it would be Big Mama. You and Frank look beat. Give me time to get out of these glad rags and I'll be back to spell you."

Before I could protest she was gone. And my protestations would have been mighty feeble. She was back just as my watch came up, dressed in ski pants and a poncho.

"Don't forget, I'm a horse lover from way back," she said as she tucked me under a blanket on the couch in the den. "Just you close your peepers and Frank and I will keep Big Mama on the move. I'll call you when it's time for breakfast."

I opened my mouth to assure Joan that I had no intention of falling asleep, but as I did I felt my eyes close and the next thing I knew it was morning.

At the table in front of the fireplace Joan sat puffing her cigarette and playing solitaire.

When I sat up she raised a card in greeting and as she did we heard a wild hallooing outside the house. We sprinted for the back door, flung it open and there was Frank, standing in a radiance of sunlight, leading Big Mama and grinning triumphantly.

"She just had a normal B.M.," he cried. "Big Mama just had a B.M.!"

We all ran to examine that which Big Mama had brought forth.

"Hooray!" shouted Joan.

"Thank heaven!" I breathed.

Our joy knew no bounds.

It was a beautiful, glistening stool. Copious, odious, normal in every way; a sight to gladden the heart of any horse lover.

I washed up, made a big mess of cornbread, and we all swapped horse yarns over breakfast.

From that time on Big Mama became even more of a pet. The horse that gives you the most trouble, like the baby that gives you the most trouble, always manages to get the most love.

As Dan Patch reached adolescence we slowly began to realize that he was different in manner, temperament, disposition, and rate of growth from any colt we'd ever raised.

For one thing, he was soon larger than all the other colts foaled that spring and on his first birthday could easily have passed for a two-year-old. But for all his great size Dan was not ungraceful. He was properly proportioned, retained his good head, and managed to achieve a fleshiness that kept him from looking raw-boned.

He also had shed his baby coat and was now a rich, burnished, liver chestnut, like his ma, with a luxuriant flaxen mane and tail.

But Dan showed absolutely no signs of "studdiness"—the quality of masculine aggressiveness that most stallions display as yearlings.

The other colts nipped him; kicked him; shoved him away from the hay bin; usurped his place at the watering trough. He was definitely low man in horse pecking order.

In spite of his companions' boorish conduct, Dan Patch refused to fight back. In a battle of wills with the other horses he would quietly step aside and turn the other cheek (or flank, as the case might be), always remaining a gentleman.

When it came time to start him on his colt's training schedule, Frank tried to circle him at the end of a longue rein but soon found that no amount of whip cracking or vocal exhortation could persuade Dan to move any faster than a walk.

Joan Benson, intrigued by his placid disposition, decided to buy him with the intention of eventually teaching him to jump.

"Since it's impossible to excite him, he may make a wonderful jumper. I think I'll work with him a while and see what happens," she said.

What happened was that Dan followed Joan around like a dog, licked her hand sloppily whenever she came near him, and stood soulful-eyed at the gate, waiting for her to return to give him his next lesson.

Within a few months Dan began to show promise as a jumper,

but there was one thing about him that puzzled Joan as it did us: he had absolutely no interest in horses of the opposite sex.

The other studs, some far younger than Dan, had begun to strike up friendships with the little girl colts. And whenever the fillies came in season these eager little fellows would curl their noses, scent the air, and whinny excitedly.

But not Dan!

For his companion, Dan chose another stud colt.

If the fillies nuzzled up to him flirtatiously Dan quietly moved away.

Finally Joan asked the vet to examine him.

"Remarkable! Remarkable!" muttered the vet when he completed his examination.

Frank, Joan and I waited in trepidation, not really wanting to hear the verdict.

"This colt has no male sex organs!" exclaimed the vet. "Most remarkable thing I've ever seen. I've read about cases like this but I never thought I'd actually meet up with one. Well, for one thing, you won't have to pay to have him gelded!"

He chuckled heartily and since there didn't seem to be much else that we could do, we soon joined him.

"Would you like the money back that you paid for Dan?" Frank asked Joan after the vet had gone.

"No. I had no intention of breeding him," she said gallantly. "This shouldn't interefere with his performance as a jumper. But he does behave very strangely."

A single word described Dan. The word MEEK.

Like mother, like son, we told ourselves. Wasn't Big Mama the soul of meekness?

A mare with such a saintly character should certainly be allowed one aberration . . .

Then Big Mama produced her next foal. Frank and I took one look at it and summoned the vet in a hurry—the same vet who examined Dan. We brought Big Mama's foal out for inspection. A beautiful little critter; dark bay with one white point; fine-boned; bright-eyed; a sweet and perfect filly . . . or was it?

The vet shook his head, baffled.

Big Mama's young-un had a bag so she must have started out to be a filly. But she also had rudimentary *male* sex organs, so you could also say she started out to be a stud.

"You've got a crazy mixed-up mare there," said the vet.

We looked at Big Mama, standing huge, silent—and, as usual, meek and morose—beside her new colt.

"And I paid a crazy mixed-up price for her breeding," groaned Frank. "What do you do in a case like this?" he asked the vet.

"Well you could have all sorts of fancy operations later on; cost you more than the horse would be worth—or, you could name Big Mama's offspring Christine and forget the whole thing!"

And that's just what we did.

"Do you think we'll ever be able to sell Big Mama's child?" I asked Frank as Christine ripened into manhood (womanhood?).

My question was answered a few days later when a young girl appeared at the ranch looking for a colt she could break.

"I can't pay much for it," she said. "But I can trade."

The girl, who was tall, fair-haired, and painfully thin, reached in her jeans and brought out a blue velvet box. She opened it and sunlight sparkled on a tiny engagement ring and a matching wedding band.

"My boyfriend changed his mind about getting married when I told him I want to study to be a vet," she said. "He let me keep these. Can I trade them for the filly?"

"It's a deal," cried Frank, scarcely glancing at the tiny stones. "I'll trade for anything that doesn't eat."

"Ohh, I'm so happy!" cried the girl, flinging her arms around Christine's neck and burying her nose in her mane. "I'll go get my trailer and be right back after her."

"Just a minute." Frank stopped her as she bent double to

slip inside her Volkswagen. "There's something you should know about this . . . er . . . filly. She isn't really a filly . . ."

The girl backed out of the car and stood up. Her pale, myopic eyes widened.

"Since you're studying to be a vet, I can speak plainly," said Frank.

"Do you mean she isn't sound?"

"Oh she's sound all right. Only . . . well . . ." Frank lowered his voice and I saw the girl stare at Christine in astonishment.

Then she burst out laughing.

"Wait till I tell my animal husbandry teacher about this!" she cried. "With a colt like this I can make veterinarian history!" She bent to get in the car, then straightened up once more.

"There's something I ought to tell you," she said. "About the rings. The engagement ring has a slight flaw in it. It's only worth two hundred dollars."

As the Volkswagen sputtered down the lane, Frank shoved his hat to the back of his head and grinned wickedly.

"That's what I call a good trade," he said. "Wedding rings from a dame who won't mate, in exchange for a filly who can't!"

"Oh stop sounding so smug and shriven just because you and that horse-sick girl managed to bare your imperfections. What in the world are we going to do with a spare set of wedding rings?"

Little did I know that fate had the answer.

When our son, B.G., enlisted in the Navy he managed to get himself engaged every time he came home on leave, a luxury he'd never have been able to afford without Frank's trade-in wedding rings.

2
Johnny,
Who Was Mighty Nice With Rice

At the Bar None it is impossible to get along without ranch help and impossible to get along with it. We have discovered that it is mostly the peripheral people who look for ranch work: the wanderers, the dreamers, the misfits. Those bored by indoor labor, those bored by outdoor labor, and those simply bored.

We have an endless parade of such workers.

All arrive at the ranch wide-eyed, eager and broke. All become disgruntled and discontented the instant they have money in their jeans. We know this, but we still always become involved with them personally. We listen to their problems, attempt to solve them. In turn they appear to love us, but in the span of a pay day they leave us.

The first hand to join our happy family at the Bar None was Johnny, a dapper, smiling Philippino. Although hired for outdoor work Johnny fancied himself a chef. He inspected the kitchen cupboards and clucked unhappily because he found so little rice.

"Need rots of lice," he said. "Make plenty fine dishes."

32

I promptly stocked up on rice and Johnny proved true to his word. He made fried rice, boiled rice, baked rice, Spanish rice, Chile Rice, Rice pudding (with and without raisins), chicken and rice, shrimp and rice, peppers and rice, and pineapple and rice. And to go with the rice he made floods of gravy.

One day I caught him testing the consistency of the gravy by dipping four fingers in it and sucking them lustily.

"Johnny! That's unsanitary!" I cried.

"Not unsanitaly! Only way to test glavy!" he retorted indignantly. "You test with spoon other chef he use same spoon. You test with fingers no one else use same fingers."

The logic was incontrovertible.

Having taken over the duties of the kitchen Johnny next assumed the role of gardener. In all the years we've lived at the Bar None neither Frank nor I has ever tried to grow anything but cactus because the gophers don't like cactus. Everything else they devour as fast as it's put in the ground. But Johnny had ten green thumbs when it came to reviving drooping and neglected plants. As he dug and sweated, cigarette dangling from his mouth, eyes squinted against the curling smoke, he told us about some of the other places he'd worked.

Within an hour I counted nineteen kinds of jobs Johnny had held in forty-two states. Privately I began to wonder how long we could expect him to stay on his present job, and glancing at Frank, I could tell from his expression that he was wondering the same thing.

Johnny was captivatingly courteous and diligent. He wore a neat little white house coat and always addressed me as "Madame" with the French accent. It really was a novelty to be called "Madame" at the Bar None.

After Johnny had been with us a week Frank and I had to go away for an entire day so Frank gave Johnny sufficient spending money to tide him over in case some emergency arose before we got back. We were so confident of Johnny's honesty and reliability that we decided to stay away over night.

The next afternoon when we got back Frank and I reached

the back door at the same moment and burst into the kitchen together.

"Johnny?" I called eagerly.

No answer.

We weren't alarmed because we had talked to Johnny on the phone the night before and he assured us we could stay away a month if we wanted to. He said he'd manage nicely without us.

"He's probably out back." I said, when Frank called him and got no reply.

Just then the door of the kitchen opened and Johnny appeared. He wore crumpled slacks, a noticeably soiled, flamboyant sport shirt and was barefoot. His fringe of black hair stood straight up in the air; his eyes were red-rimmed and glazed and a sour odor emanated from him.

Could this be our dapper and debonair Johnny?

He lurched forward, lost his balance, and, in an effort to regain it, flung an arm around my shoulder. I tried to pull away, almost asphyxiated by the fumes of his breath.

"Hello, Rrrrrrr-uby," he said, companionably, rolling his "R" in the Philippino manner. He teetered back and forth, still with his arm around me.

"Where'd you get the booze, Johnny?" asked Frank.

"At shtore," Johnny answered, referring to a tiny market that served the ranchers, a few miles from us.

"I'll take you in town as soon as you pack," said Frank, laughing at my discomfiture as I tried vainly to extricate myself from Johnny's embrace.

"Al-leady packed," said Johnny happily. "Al-leady packed."

As Frank drove our first ranch hand away in the Camino, Johnny leaned out the window and touched his forehead in a regal salaam. "Goodbye, Rrrrrrr-uby," he called, and his little brown face was split in half by his grin.

I went back to the wine-soaked kitchen and began gathering up pans full of rice.

I carried it out to the chickens.

3

Jonathan,
the Profligate Polygamist

Jonathan is the ranch rooster. Skeet, the ranch foreman, returned to the Bar None after a day off, carrying Jonathan in
a packing case.

Jonathan had belonged to Skeet's sister who lived in a section
of the San Fernando Valley where poultry were being zoned
out. Reluctantly she had to part with her pet and so Skeet
assured her he would have a happy home on our ranch.

At the age of two Jonathan had never set foot outside his
packing case. He had never scratched for worms; never taken
a dust bath; never seen a hen, much less flirted with one. But
even through the slats of his packing case we could see that
Jonathan was no ordinary rooster.

He was magnificent.

A cross between a Black Minorca and a Golden Bantam
fighting cock, Jonathan boasted an irridescent, emerald-black
coat, overlaid with marblings of the purest bright gold. He
had a flaming red comb that stood four inches high and fiery
red wattles that quivered like a judge's jowls at every step.

We wondered what Jonathan would do when he saw Winifred,

our lissome White Wyandotte hen. And we soon found out. Winifred happened by just as Skeet pulled the last nail out of the packing case and turned Jonathan loose.

Instantly Jonathan rendered Winifred's eggs fertile!

The first hen he'd ever seen!

Winifred was followed by Granville, our dolorous guinea cock. As soon as Jonathan spied Granville he seized him by the comb, flipped him on his back and pinned him to the ground.

One feminine conquest, one masculine triumph in the first thirty seconds of play.

Cheers went up from all around. Jonathan had won unanimous acceptance at the ranch.

Winifred lost her heart to Jonathan at their first romantic encounter. Here was a relationship that the sex educators would heartily endorse. Winifred, submissive, self-effacing, feminine. Jonathan aggressive, demanding, masculine. Dr. Popenoe himself would have predicted long years of domestic tranquility.

But that's because he doesn't know Frank.

Frank decided we weren't making proper use of Jonathan's special talents. "A rooster," he informed me, "should have a flock."

"But Winifred is happy with things the way they are."

"You are anthropomorphic toward animals," said my husband, the rancher. "On a ranch this is impossible. You must be realistic. Every animal must make a contribution to the ranch economy."

I married this man because I wanted to live the life of a realistic rancher and not an anthropomorphic writer, so I shut up.

The next time Frank went to town he returned with two hens. Golden Buff Orpingtons. Brash, bold biddies without conscience or character.

The minute they saw Jonathan they ruffled their feathers, uttered soft, throaty gurgles and cocked their heads archly.

Immediately Jonathon rendered their eggs fertile. Both of them. Right in front of Winifred.

From then on Henny and Penny, the two heartless hussies, attached themselves to Jonathan, and Winifred became *persona non grata*.

If she falteringly attempted to approach Jonathan he would fly at her and drive her away.

This continued for several days and then Winifred disappeared.

Frank laughed at the intensity of my search for her. He laughed still more when I found her, under the horse trailer, quietly, patiently and, I expect self-righteously, sitting on a clutch of eggs.

"Oh, this is too much!" I cried.

"No, it isn't enough," Frank corrected, as he counted the eggs under Winifred. "She could sit on six more, at least."

And my callous rancher of a husband then proceeded to slip six more eggs beneath Winifred: three from each of the heartless hussies.

I looked at Winifred and looked away hastily before she could return my look. My heart ached for her. For her and every misguided female betrayed by a male. It wasn't sufficiently degrading for her to sit on the eggs of that philanderer, Jonathan. Now she faced the thankless and humiliating task of hatching the eggs of his concubines!

Hunt, hunt, hunt.
Peck, peck, peck.
Scratch, scratch, scratch.
Cluck, cluck, cluck.
Repeat from the top.

This is the pattern of Jonathan's day. A day which starts, at the first blush of dawn, with a series of ear-splitting crows, delivered within three feet of our bedroom window.

Like most early risers, Jonathan is impatient with those

who sleep late and does what he can to annoy them. I've decided that's why he always crows fifteen crows in a row, without stopping. It's because he figures by the fifteenth crow sleep is effectually routed.

Though a polygamist, wife-beater, braggart and pan-handler, Jonathan knows how to keep his harem happy. Whenever he finds an especially juicy worm, a choice kernel of grain, or a delicious cool bit of lettuce, he always summons the hens, then steps aside gallantly, allowing them to enjoy their fill of it before he so much as touches a morsel.

His thoughful hunt and peck missions continue all morning. Then the hens are inspired to lay their eggs.

They discreetly withdraw to the privacy of their hayshed while engaged in this feminine occupation, and Jonathan, taking advantage of the lull that follows, usually sneaks a little shut-eye.

He settles low in the dust, allows his beak to fall forward till it rests on his burnished gold breast; then, with head low, and wings outstretched he appears like a tired, aging film actor, who has let down his guard between takes.

But once the hens come cackling forth, proclaiming to the world the miracle they have performed, Jonathan springs erect and crows lustily, expressing a pride and enthusiam out of all proportion to his part in the performance.

Jonathan learned quickly that food is dispensed from the back door at meal times. He's not the only mendicant on the ranch who has made this discovery. But he always manages to reach the door ahead of the ranch cats, the ground squirrels, and the blue jays; Lady, the ranch dog; and Belinda, our feisty feline.

I'm sure Jonathan has an inner radar that tells him when food is on its way from the table to the door because any time I open the back door I see him streak across the yard at breakneck speed head outthrust, his body rolling in a washerwoman's waddle. Usually he catches the first potato paring or bread crust before it hits the ground. Then he stands with outstretched wings, waiting for the hens to sample it.

The dogs and cats sit by, sullen and skulking. They'd like to throttle Jonathan but they have tasted the sharpness of his beak and learned the hard way to respect his spurs, so they remain glowering on the sidelines until he has stuffed his craw before they move in for the crumbs.

Throughout the day at the Bar None—as I hang out the wash, pour leftover dish water down the gopher holes, or sit quietly polishing tack—I frequently get the feeling that someone is watching me.

And someone is.

My good friend, Jonathan.

Jonathan watches me greedily, quizzically, circumspectly. Not because he is personally interested in me, but because I am a food symbol. If I bring my sewing outdoors and become absorbed in the turn of a seam, any time I look up for a moment, there's Jonathan, one leg raised, his bright, beady eye riveted on me. If I stretch out, as I sometimes do, beneath the live oaks, hoping to nap for a while between fly bites, I hear a soft "plop," and there's Jonathan, striding hastily away from the chicken doo he has dropped within inches of my head. At other times Jonathan waits till I doze off, then he lets out an ear-splitting crow, within a hair's span of my ear.

I have learned something about Jonathan's crow, listening to it, as I am forced to, from closeup. After the first raucous blast there is an after-crow. A soft, sighing, sibillant susurrus that sounds as if a bellows were taking in air. I'm told a bird's windpipe stretches for yards within its chest cavity in a series of intricate convolutions, and I imagine it is the hidden recesses that are filled with air during the after-crow.

Seeing Jonathan's round, yellow eye glaring at me from leafy ambush can be a mighty unsettling experience. But I find it more disconcerting to awaken from a siesta on a hot afternoon to discover him roosting beside me on the redwood lounge. He looks at me. I look at him. Questions go unanswered between us. We have a mutual, healthy respect for each other, but unfortunately there are barriers of communication that we seem unable to surmount and so we find ourselves unable to establish a deeper rapprochement.

There are days when the sun clamps a hot, brassy lid on the ranch and we cook under it, along with the sage.

On such days Jonathan stands with eyes glazed (but still riveted on me), panting and holding his wings away from his body in a desperate attempt to trap any passing air current. Pink skin shows where his feathers have moulted and he looks as if he were out in his ragged pink bloomers. It makes me feel warm just to look at him and I move to the shadow of the cottonwoods, hoping to get away from him. But he follows me there, standing first one one foot, then the other, his expression accusing. The implication he makes is that I am responsible for his discomfort.

I stare at him. He stares back.

We alternately doze and blink.

On Castro Peak, the highest point of the surrounding range, the fire lookout has his eye trained on both of us, watching for the first curl of smoke that tells him the thick brush covering the mountains has become so hot that it has spontaneously ignited itself.

But before the chapparal goes up in flames, the wind shifts. An ocean breeze slips through the canyons and the temperature drops. This is the blessed mid-afternoon weather change we have been waiting for.

Jonathan lowers his wings, settles his feathers and casts his eye about, looking for a hen.

I know what he is thinking. And when Jonathan is seized with a romantic notion he is like a husband I once read about in a marriage case history who would drag his wife away from whatever she was doing, even if she were basting a roast, to throw her on the bed and have his way with her.

Jonathan is just as subtle in his approach to the hens. Spotting one, he heads for her with the speed of a bullet, seizes her by the comb, hops astride her, and renders her eggs fertile before she has time to cackle a protest.

The hens display a remarkable aplomb in coping with the situation. They rise, settle their feathers, utter a sub-vocal expletive, and go on about their business.

Jonathan makes his rounds at least once a day, usually in the mid-morning hours, then returns to stake-out. Whenever I go inside to prepare a meal, he plants himself outside the kitchen door. Thus, when I emerge with the table scraps, he manages to get an edge on the guineas.

When Frank and I finish the day-end chores and settle down for a smoke and a chat, Jonathan is right beside us, the yellow eye round and watching.

This is the good part of day when the purple shadows of the mountains spread like stains across the valley and the night air rushes in sweet and fresh from the sea.

As the blue dusk of twilight deepens Jonathan eventually hops to his roost, there to be joined by the concubines. They preen and prattle, settle down for the night, and last of all, Jonathan tucks his head under his wing. This is when I give a sigh of relief. The bright yellow eye will not be on me till tomorrow . . .

There was a client like Jonathan, back in the Squirrel Cage. His name was Arrowsmith Lippincott and he would happily seize a secretary by the comb if the right opportunity presented itself. He was advertising manager of an orange juice account and orange juice flowed in his veins. Because of this his eyes were yellow. He used to fix his jaundiced glance on me in client meetings, exactly like Jonathan. But there the resemblance ended. Arrowsmith Lippincott was much too tight with a budget to underwrite even one concubine.

4

The Senoritas Were Genteel
for Real

"Here's an ad that says you can get a refined, educated, and mature Latin woman as a housekeeper for a little over a hundred dollars a month," I told Frank, one evening. I was engaged in my favorite pastime: reading the classified section.

"What do they mean by a 'Latin woman'?"

"A woman from South America, I believe."

I was hedging.

"Does that mean she speaks English?"

"Well . . . not exactly. It says she speaks Spanish."

"You mean you want to hire someone we can't even communicate with?" cried Frank. In his violence he almost swallowed his pipe and this kept him from going further.

"What difference does it make if she doesn't speak English if she's mature, refined, and reliable?"

The pipe was coughed loose with a snort.

"It makes a big difference to me. I don't speak Spanish!"

"You don't have to. I remember some high-school Spanish. It's certainly worth investigating. The salary's so low. Please?"

"What if you're not here and I have to tell her something?"

"You can make out with sign language. Please, honey? It would be so great to have someone to help me with the cooking and cleaning . . ."

I accepted silence for consent and the next day began the process of obtaining a refined, mature Latin woman as a housekeeper for the Bar None. In doing so I discovered that obtaining a Latin housekeeper did involve serious investigations —of us. We could have adopted a baby more readily.

After we signed innumerable affidavits testifying to our sobriety, high moral caliber, and solvency, we paid a month's salary in advance as a pledge of good faith to the employment agency furnishing said housekeeper; put up an additional month's salary as "termination pay"; promised to allow our housekeeper half a day off every week; agreed to see that she found transportation to church every Sunday, and stated that we had no objection to her visiting or receiving visits from relatives. This last proviso seemed rather silly since we were told that our housekeeper-to-be came from the lower extremity of Mexico —not from South America, as we had been led to believe— and we couldn't imagine how she would visit relatives or have them visit her if they lived almost a thousand miles away! (Ahh, naivete, thy name is Griffith!)

Finally we arrived at the culmination of all these solemn vows and promises and were told that we could meet our Senorita.

Tense and emotionally depleted after more than ten weeks of harrowing negotiations, Frank and I sat in the lush anteroom of the employment agency that dealt in Latin ladies and waited for Mina Sanches de la Montez to be ushered in.

We cooled our heels for twenty agonized minutes, both silently mulling over our misgivings and regrets, before a door opened and the coldly beautiful Mexican senora who ran the agency appeared leading TWO tiny, smiling Latin ladies, both dressed in neat, restrained black.

The sight of two mature, demure ladies undid us.

Which was ours?

Did we have a choice?

Were we to get two for the price of one?

The mystery was solved when they were presented to us as sisters.

One, Mina, the slightly older of the two, was to work for us. The other, Chole, her fragile, sweet-faced sister, was to work for a neighboring rancher.

We were advised that the two sisters were inseparable and inordinately fond of each other and could not possibly be expected to remain on any job unless allowed to see each other at least once a week.

It seemed such a harmless request that we readily agreed to it. How could we do otherwise? The mere thought of being apart from each other for seven days caused both dainty sisters to dissolve in tears. They kissed each other; they kissed the handsome Senora who ran the employment agency; they kissed us. Then Chole was led from the room and Mina, complete with shiny black plastic suitcase, was ours!

There was no doubt that Mina was both mature and refined. She stood slender and erect in spite of her forty years. Her face had a proud, patrician cast to it; her stance held an unassailable dignity that made us feel like unworthy peons in her presence.

She liked her room, which I had painted in warm earth tones sparked with tangerine, and when she had hung her crucifix over her bed she seemed instantly to take possession of it.

Slipping into a trim black lace dress, she indicated that she was ready to assume her duties. Since I mostly wear jeans and sweaters at the ranch, I felt much better equipped to do the menial work than Mina, for it seemed a pity to let her soil such an elegant dress. Therefore I motioned her to relax at the window while I got dinner.

Naturally we expected Mina to eat with us and she gracefully accepted her position at the table. Dinner conversation was noticeably constrained since Mina could speak no English; I didn't trust myself to attempt a conversation in high-school Spanish; and Frank had no intention of addressing Mina under any circumstances—that was our understanding when he agreed to hire her.

As soon as the meal was over, Frank headed for the sanctuary of his den and I washed the dishes, allowing Mina to dry them. The elegant black lace dress had wrist length sleeves with ruffles and I couldn't ask her to desecrate them by dunking them in dishwater.

When the dishes were done Mina curtsied, murmured: "Buenas noches," which I understood to mean "good night," and retired to her room. Within ten minutes her light was turned off and she was asleep. I attributed her early retirement to exhaustion after a first day in a strange home. But it turned out that Mina always went to bed at dusk.

The next morning she appeared in a chic and svelte flowered dress, also with long ruffled sleeves. Her hair lay in neat, ear-hugging wings against the finely modeled hollows of her cheeks. Pearl earrings glowed at her ears and she wore nylon stockings and high heeled shoes.

I had intended to give the house a walloping cleaning with her assistance and so I came to breakfast in shredded jeans and one of Frank's old paint shirts with my hair swathed in a towel to keep the dust out.

One look at Mina in her handsome feminine apparel convinced me that I couldn't possibly ask her to mop floors or wash windows. And I couldn't ask her to change her clothes for something better suited to housecleaning—I didn't know enough Spanish.

Fortunately Frank had already started his ranch chores so he couldn't see that the mistress of the house was doing the housecleaning while the housekeeper watched in trim elegance, a condescending little smile on her lips.

But just in case Frank should come in before lunch, I gave Mina a job. I had her paste my blue chip stamps in their books. She was a whizz at it. And since I'm quite a whizz at house-cleaning, I had everything squared away and ship shape by the time Frank returned for lunch.

I wondered if Mina could cook. She certainly wasn't cut out for housework. Her hands looked as if she had never done anything more strenuous in her life than gather rose petals.

She made a complete change of wardrobe twice a day and her clothing was immaculate and remained so, since I found it impossible to ask her to do anything demeaning.

After one look at that calm, assured countenance—every feature composed, eyebrows raised delicately—I couldn't bring myself to ask Mina to do anything. In fact, I felt like a frump who should be apologizing for my appearance. My hair, in comparison with Mina's, looked unkempt. My hands were the hands of a peasant. My clothing was gauche. If I had asked her to wipe the dust off the buffet I would have felt as if I were a scullery maid commanding a queen.

But even royalty cooks. It is an art that the noblest need not be ashamed of. Besides, I had to go in town to be gone all day so Mina would have to cook for Frank. There was a frantic three-way conversation between Mina, the Spanish-English dictionary and me. The result was that I felt reasonably certain that Mina understood she must feed my "esposo" while I was away. She smiled her cool, aloof smile and gave a con-descending curtsy.

Before my courage failed I left for town. About the middle of the afternoon I could stand it no longer. Was Frank fainting from hunger? I had to know. He is a man who likes to be fed; regularly. He will forgive anything except tardiness at meal-time. He answered the phone and immediately I sensed that he was in a state of panic bordering on hysteria.

First there was a string of expletives.

Good. This would let off most of the steam.

The expletives were followed by a roar.

"Get home and get this woman away from me! She's already fed me four meals and expects me to start on my fifth. Every time she sees me she prepares another meal. I've had steak and potatoes, chile and tortillas, eggs and spinach and chicken and cabbage. Now she's making pork chops and rice."

Apparently Mina could cook.

When Frank put her on the phone I found that under the stress of emergency it is possible to call to mind a great deal of high school Spanish.

"*No mas comido para Senor,* Mina!" I commanded.

"Si, Senora," she replied in her gentle, polished tones, and I felt like an oaf for raising my voice to her.

"If only I knew the secret," I thought. The secret of Mina's indomitable gentility.

The employer of Mina's sister, Chole, lived on a ranch a few miles from us. She phoned to say that Chole was pining for a glimpse of her sister and asked if we could arrange to bring them together.

Since we can't leave the ranch on weekends because that is when prospective customers come to look at the horses, we told our neighbor to bring Chole over Friday night and we'd be happy to have her stay with us till Monday when she could call for her again.

Before we knew it, Mrs. Davis, our neighbor, arrived with Chole, a tiny, genteel replica of Mina. Chole stood smiling and bowing, attired in black lace; white gloves spotless; trim shoes sparkling; her hair in a fashionable pouf; shiny black plastic suitcase at her side.

The reunion of the two dainty ladies was touching. They kissed each other, clasped hands, then wandered off together and remained inseparable for the rest of the weekend.

How could I possibly interrupt such a tender tryst with a

crass request for help with the housework? The answer is, I couldn't. So I shooed Mina and Chole on their way and cooked all the meals and did all the cleaning myself.

The fact that each meal was more elaborate than the last and that all courses were varied and intricate just shows how desperately I attempted to impress my distinguished house guests. Mina and Chole adored and appreciated everything I did for them; and to show their appreciation, they produced a box of exquisite hand-embroidered handkerchiefs which they insisted I accept as a gift.

Monday morning when Chole departed I was bone tired and decide to ask Mina to help with the dusting. But she pleaded a headache, retired to her room and remained there the rest of the day.

The following weekend when Chole reappeared on the scene and she and Mina fell on each other's necks, my eye met Frank's. There was such fire in his that I looked away quickly. But he caught me finishing the last of the supper dishes by myself and cornered me.

"Well?"

No need to say more. We both knew what the question portended.

"We signed a contract," I reminded him.

"Does that mean you have to remain a slave to the little princesses forever?"

"Only till the contract expires."

"And when will that be?"

"I think there's an out-clause at the end of ten weeks."

"You'll be dead by that time."

"I think that's an optimistic estimate."

I wondered if there were any legal way of wiggling out of our agreement sooner. But as it turned out we didn't have to. Mina came to me the next day and explained in remarkably fluent English that she and Chole wished to visit their brother in Hemet the following weekend.

So! Here we thought they were lone, lorn critters—strangers in a strange land—and they had a brother in Hemet. And Mina could speak English. Anger was replaced by hope as it occurred to me that the trip to Hemet would mean that Mina and Chole would be out of our hair for two whole days.

Then a dreadful thought struck me.

"Do we have to take you to Hemet?" I asked, speaking in English, since Mina obviously undertood it.

"My brother will come for us," she replied.

Her brother arrived in an old but presentable Cadillac. Apparently he was one of the working members of the family, for he wore grubby jeans; his hands were earth-stained and calloused and his brow furrowed with care. However, he assisted his two dainty sisters into the Cadillac as if he were transporting royal blood. After they had pulled away I allowed myself the luxury of sitting idle for awhile; something I had not been able to do since Mina's arrival.

Suddenly a glorious thought occurred to me. I jumped up, inspired by it, and ran to Mina's room where I threw open the door to her closet. It was empty. Chests and bureau likewise.

When I joined Frank at the corrals I wore a smile that wouldn't come off.

"What's with you?" he asked, responding to my unspoken ebullience with a married man's radar.

"I have a secret!" I smirked.

"Bully for you. Let me know when you burst trying to keep it a secret."

"The princesses aren't coming back!"

Frank first looked hopeful, then incredulous.

"How do you know?"

"They took all their things with them."

Frank lifted a shovel full of manure and swung it within inches of me.

"You're covered with luck, girl," he said. "Better not push it. No more help for a while. Right?"

5

Winifred, a Woman Wronged

Jonathan's desertion of Winifred made me feel responsible for her and her brood. Every few hours, all day long, I would peer under the horse trailer to see how things were going with her. She remained on the nest all day. But in the cool of the evening she came off for a little water and a few grains of corn. Then she'd give each egg a delicate half-turn and settle down again.

"How long before the baby chicks arrive?"

I asked this question at least once a day.

"Twenty-one days is the usual incubation period for chickens," Frank would reply matter-of-factly. He didn't share my fine eagerness for a glimpse of the little ones.

Would they take after Winifred?

Or Jonathan?

Or the hussies! This was a horrible thought!

By the twentieth day I was down on my hands and knees every few minutes trying to see what was going on under the trailer. Winifred was thoroughly annoyed with me and had taken to pecking at me.

On the morning of the twenty-first day I suddenly remembered the foxes. We have so many of them on the ranch. I ran to Frank and begged him to build a shelter for the chicks. And though he swears he isn't anthropomorphic about animals he dropped what he was doing and built one for me. A cage that had formerly housed an injured racoon was hauled out of the shed, hastily repaired and covered with fine mesh screening. Next we lined it with fresh clean hay and stocked it with water and grain.

My visits to Winifred's retreat became more frequent. In spite of her scoldings and peckings I peered under her wings. There was neither chick nor child. Two days passed. Someone had miscalculated; as often happens with a new bride.

We were in the midst of the summer's worst heat wave. The temperature hovered at a hundred in the shade and tempers grew short, especially Winifred's.

What if the eggs weren't fertile? This hadn't occurred to me before. Jonathan's eggs not fertile? Impossible!

By this time Winifred's comb had turned pale and flaccid. She had shed most of her feathers and her bumpy skin showed in a dozen places. She panted constantly. And whenever I tried to slip an egg out from under her to get a closer look at it, she'd reach out with her beak and deftly twirl it back under her wings.

"Relax," Frank counseled, as he saw me head for the horse trailer for the eighth time since sun-up. "The chicks aren't here yet, the eggs haven't pipped!"

"Pipped?"

"The chick inside the egg has to peck open the shell. It's called pipping."

"Oh!" This was a revelation to me. I'd never even stopped to think how the new chick gets out of his nursery.

I sat down as close as I could to the horse trailer, in a little lace doily of shade cast by a tall Chinese Elm.

The temperature registered a hundred and eight in the shade where there was a slight breeze. What must the temperature be under Winifred?

Maybe the chicks would cook inside the shell!

Just then I heard a small flurry. I dropped to my knees beside Winifred. Peering from beneath her wings was a little golden head with two beady-bright eyes. I screamed to Frank, and, as I watched, a tiny ball of golden fluff staggered out from under Winifred's wing. It was followed by a second identical fluff ball.

Both chicks were black with little yellow capuchin caps on their heads.

Frank was beside me now, grinning a fatuous grin that smacked greatly of anthropomorphism.

Gently he lifted the weak but cantankerous Winifred off her nest.

"There's one pipping!"

Sure enough it was!

Right before our eyes a small hole appeared in the shell of one of the eggs and we heard the tiniest sound in the world: the sound of pipping.

Completely unaware of the heat, I sat enthralled. Sweat poured down my face, ran down my back; I was oblivious to it.

Slowly, between long pauses, the chick inside the egg gathered strength, the pipping grew louder and more determined and at last a crack extended completely around the egg.

While this was going on, Winifred fussed and fumed and clucked and cackled. And the two downy chicks, suddenly exhibiting phenomenal strength, dodged and darted around her.

Then the pipped shell fell apart, revealing inside a wet little monster that resembled a miniature pterodactyl. It's gluey head and plastered body were coiled in a foetal position. Only the head apparently had accomplished the pipping. But as the hot air dried the little creature's feathers, it soon rose up on its toothpick legs and became another downy chick; white, with black wing-tips; an exact replica of Winifred.

Five chicks hatched out that blistering, broiling day. Two blacks and three whites. The others were too pooped to pip and didn't make it.

Over the protests of Winifred, who had suddenly become all

mother, we placed her and the little ones in the cage we had prepared for them. Then, just to make certain that predators wouldn't get to them, we lifted the cage onto a table we had placed in the shade of a live oak tree. Here Winifred could watch her brood and savor the sweet canyon breezes, if there happened to be any.

We felt as exhausted as Winifred looked after the ordeal of delivery and sat, sipping iced tea and watching the animated fluff balls for at least an hour, knowing all the while that the chores were waiting.

Winifred pretended to be annoyed at our presence but actually she was pleased and proud to show off her offspring. She drank vast quantities of water, scratched at the grain we gave her, and showed the baby chicks how they, too, must scratch if they wanted to make their way in the world. Then she nestled down and hid all of them under her wings. All that showed beneath her was an orderly row of tiny feet.

Our responsibilities increased rather than diminished as the little chicks grew. Every day we cleaned out the cage, put in fresh water and grain and gave Winifred a cool leaf of lettuce.

She would cluck and complain and call her chicks under her wings whenever we came near her, but secretly she seemed pleased to know that her babies were safe from the foxes.

It soon became apparent that Winifred's quarters were cramped. The chicks lost their fluffy down, sprouted vestigial wings and would pile up on Winifred's back in a four-stack pyramid.

Winifred rolled her eyes at us pitifully whenever they lined up astride her like Japanese television gymnasts and eventually we got her message. We overturned the cage and allowed Winifred and her family to run free all day. But we insisted that they return to their quarters at night.

This meant that every evening, at dusk, I had the job of luring Winifred and the chicks into their dormitory.

It became an elaborate and exhausting ritual. First I put grain in the cage where it rested on the ground; then I'd hold up one corner of the cage (it had no bottom) and call: "Here, chick, chick, chick, chick, chick."

At the first "chick" Jonathan and the hussies, with the guineas in hot pursuit, would tear toward the cage and Winifred and the chicks would wind up in the rear. Holding the cage, fighting off the impostors and trying to guide Winifred and the moppets safely inside required pretzel-like dexterity. I'd capture the chicks, lift the cage to ensnare Winnie and the chicks would get out. Then I'd coax Winnie inside, lift a corner of the cage again and as the chicks pranced in, Winifred would slip out.

After a few nights of this I decided the foxes could have the chicks. They were no longer fluff balls but had grown gangly-legged and ornery. They would stand eye to eye and beak to beak, wings extended, like wrestlers poised for a death grip. If they were that grown-up they could roost outside and tucking them into bed at night would be Winnie's problem.

Frank and I watched Winifred put on her floor show every night from our seat beneath the live oak tree. She'd hop first to the lowest rung of the corral fence, then progress to the next rung and the next. Complaining and chattering all the way, the chicks would try to follow her. Flapping, falling and flutter-ing and cheered (I almost said "egged") on by Winifred, they finally made it. Then instead of roosting properly, all in a row, as sensible chickens should, they'd try to crowd beneath Wini-fred's wings.

Since by now they were nearly as large as their mother, they lifted her completely off the fence where she'd float, in mid-air, one youngster perched between her legs, two others fighting to get under her wings and two more astraddle her back.

Helpless and humiliated, she would cluck to us appealingly but we made believe we didn't hear her.

"It's time for her to wean them," I told Frank. "She's being umbilical." Secretly I was remembering the way I felt when our son, B.G., went in the Navy and the remembrance caused me to feel a suffering kinship with Winnie.

"Loose them and let them go," I told her, one day when we were alone together. "It's tough but something every mother has to do."

Winifred ruffled her feathers but made no other reply.

She'd done her best trying to be both a father and mother to her noisy brood and she certainly had received no help from Jonathan. He continued to ignore her, having succumbed completely to the fascination of Henny and Penny, the heartless hussies.

If the chicks wandered toward the concubines, Winifred called them back sternly. I don't believe Winifred set out to turn the youngsters against their profligate father. It's just that some things are difficult to explain to children.

As adolescents the chicks displayed individual characteristics and distinctive personalities. Andrea, the only one we were sure was a pullet because of her diminutive comb, resembled a high fashion model. Her plumage was snowy white with blacktipped tail feathers and her legs were a charcoal grey. This gave her the appearance of wearing long, ribbed stockings. She had a dove-like head, soulful dark eyes and a gentle air that was very appealing.

Of the remaining four chicks, two appeared to be Dominicks who looked as if they were in prison garb since their plumage was striped in bars of black and white. The other two were white with ruddy combs.

The question of which would be egg-layers, which roosters, became a vital subject of ranch conversation. I insisted there were three hens and two cockerels.

Frank said there were four cockerels and one hen. The controversy raged for weeks.

"It'll soon be time to eat those roosters."

"What do you mean, roosters? You can't be sure they're not hens yet."

"How long do you think it takes to be sure?"

I hadn't any idea.

"I suppose when the hens start to lay?" This seemed like a pretty good guess.

But all it brought forth from my husband was a whoop and a holler.

"That would take months. We're not going to feed four roosters just to find out which one is a hen."

"Well, won't we be able to tell when the roosters start to crow?"

"I suppose we should let four roosters crow under our window every morning, including Jonathan, which would make five."

"But there's only one rooster. The others are hens."

"What makes you so sure the others are hens?"

"Take a look at their combs."

"That's just what I'm doing. Four have combs, therefore, four are roosters."

"Winifred has a comb and she's a hen."

"Her comb is different. It doesn't grow as tall as a rooster's comb."

It was true. I noticed that the hen's combs never grew as tall as the rooster's, but I didn't intend to lose the battle on that score.

"We have four pullets and one rooster. You'll see. I saw two little protuberances on the legs of the one that's a rooster, the beginning of spurs. But the four hens don't have little protuberances."

Big guffaw.

"And besides, I asked Maria." Maria was the little Mexican girl who came to clean house for me once a week. "Maria says we have four hens and one rooster. And she ought to know. She was raised on a farm in Mexico."

Bigger guffaw.

"Maria explained that it's something about their build that lets you know which is a hen and which is a rooster. The hens are broader than the roosters."

"So the hens are broads. What does that prove?"

Biggest guffaw.

I gave up. But only for the time being. I knew the conversation would surely come up again.

But by the time it did I was vacillating.

"Y'know, honey, maybe you're right. Maybe we *have* got four roosters."

"What makes you think so?"

"Well those little proturberances—they all seem to have them."

"Why don't you ask Maria how she feels about protuberances?"

It was no use. I could see that my prognostications and divinations weren't getting me anywhere.

Some days I'd try a different tack.

"I looked at the chickens very carefully today, Frank."

"That must have been a novel experience."

"We've got four hens."

"Wanna bet?"

This sounded interesting.

"What'll you bet?"

"That we've got four roosters!"

"Oh, Frank! You know we have at least two hens. Maybe three."

"Okay, put up your bet."

"Well . . . I'm not really sure yet."

"Do you only bet on sure things?"

Actually this is true. I'm just not a gambler.

"Give me time to think a little longer." (Secretly I was hoping I'd hear a rooster crow before Frank did.)

The next day we started all over again.

"Well, are you ready to admit we've got four roosters?"

"Not ready to bet on it, if that's what you mean."

"I guess you know we're beginning to sound like prisoners betting which cockroach will get over the wall first."

We were!

"Let's forget the whole thing," I suggested magnanimously. "And raise four roosters? Not on your life!"

"They're all so cute. I couldn't bear to part with any."

Came a time when I was ready to eat those words and the chickens, too. As they grew older they took to sitting on the patio chairs and tables, on top of the clothesline, with or without clothes on it; they left their calling cards on back walk and stoop. They scratched in the flower beds, dug up the few pitiful plants I'd been nursing along for years.

But what really rocked me was Winifred's craven capitulation to Jonathan. As soon as the youngsters could fend for themselves, she went back to him. Not as his honorable spouse, but as part of his fawning entourage.

And, as if that weren't sufficiently craven, she roosted on the far side of the corral, by herself, while the heartless hussies, Henny and Penny, roosted on the opposite side of the corral, next to Jonathan.

I really consider Winifred's behavior unforgivable!

This sort of thing can result in the retrogression of an entire sex.

And besides, she did produce four roosters and only one hen.

So I lost that argument But there is a form of romantic justice. I witnessed its operation right here at the ranch.

Egbert was responsible for it.

Egbert is a sort of *Deus ex machina*. He came to us as a gift from a neighboring rancher.

A flashy White Leghorn, with an eight-point comb of bright blazing red, Egbert was raised in one of those modern setups where the chicks live in suspended cages where artificial light simulates daylight and the hens are fed round the clock and lay constantly. Confined to one of these miserable cages, much as I was confined to my Squirrel Cage, Egbert grew and grew till there wasn't any room for his comb and so it got squashed flat over one eye.

Egbert's squashed comb gave him a ribald, rakish look which, as it turned out, reflected his character.

He'd never walked on terra firma before, having swung in mid-air in his cage, so he walked with an over-extended gait that resembled a Teutonic goose step.

Egbert appeared so brow beaten (literally) you just couldn't help feeling sorry for him. And before long I found myself pampering him.

Then one day when I was bent over filling a watering trough Egbert flew into me with both spurs, catching me square in the butt. I almost jumped over the trough. From then on Egbert let me have it at least once a day. Always at an unexpected moment.

I would try to keep an eye on him whenever I worked within range of him and carried various weapons such as pitch forks, rakes, shovels, and riding crops as a means of defense. When I'd see him heading for me I'd let one fly, and if I caught him squarely, he'd withdraw to a neutral corner for another twenty-four hours.

But he was so sneaky in his maneuvers I seldom got a whack at him because he could always catch me with my guard down. I'd flick my eye at him as I went by and he'd look the other way or appear absorbed in the flavor of a juicy-pink worm; then the minute I'd turn my back he'd be on me again. He was young and his "protuberances" weren't full-grown but he could still give you a terrific belt with his beak.

What is it makes him look so wicked? I wondered about this as I walked backwards to the hay shed, endeavoring to keep an eye on him. Then I figured it out. Egbert was faceless. Between his oversize comb and his rapacious beak there was no face at all; just room for his fierce gimlet eye.

Egbert was definitely slated to become a soft bed for dumplings.

Then I made the discovery that convinced me that Eros is not thwarted in spite of the philanderings of profligate polygamists. Egbert had become Winifred's lover. She no longer followed forlornly in the wake of Jonathan and the concubines but walked proudly beside the doughty Egbert and roosted each night at his side.

Frank filed Egbert's spurs and he remained with us to start a new line of egg layers. And what a line it is. I was tracing the genealogy of Egbert's progeny the other day and found that it runs something like this.

Egbert begat Balderdash and Balderdash begat Beverly and Beverly begat Murgatroyd and Murgatroyd begat Merriweather and Merriweather begat Montmorency and Montmorency begat Millicent . . .

Of course Jonathan did some begatting, too.

Jonathan begat Joshua, Son of Jonathan, a handsome, black and gold replica of his old man; and Joshua, being just like his pappy, proved a heller with the chicks. When Joshua reached his maturity he developed those little protuberances that turn into long, shiny, switchblade spurs and as soon as he acquired his spurs Joshua also acquired every one of Egbert's young wives!

6

Spots Before Our Eyes — An
Appaloosa Adventure

"Frank, what kind of horse is that with the dark coat and spotted rump?"

"That's an Appaloosa. I think they're descended from Indian ponies."

"That's where you're wrong, mister," a drawling voice spoke up.

We were at a breeder's horse show in Simi Valley, one of the many such shows we attend constantly in order to bring young stock before the other breeders in the hope of making a sale.

We were perched on a fence rail and turned, at the sound of the voice, to see that it came from a long, lean horseman who straddled the rail next to us.

"Name's Chuck Barstow," said the stranger and shook hands with Frank.

His skin was the color of oxblood leather; his eyes crinkled by long exposure to the glare of the sun. His hair, once red, was frosted with grey. His profile, his Stetson, his stance, were all straight out of Marlboro Country. "I raise them kind of horses," he said, pointing to the flashy stud horse with the splash of color across his loins. They ain't just ordinary Indian ponies even though the Nez Perce Indians in Palouse, Washington, did figger out how to breed them spots true again. They get their name from the Palouse River. At first they were called a Palouse horse but somehow that got trampled to Appaloosa and that's what they call 'em now."

"Those spotted rumps are really spectacular," I said with honest admiration. "I don't think I've ever seen a more attractive color arrangement."

"An Appaloosa breeds that color true same as a Palomino does," said Chuck Barstow. "You breed a loud colored stud to a solid color grade mare and you get a colt with a spotted rump."

"Every time?" asked Frank, dubiously.

"Eighty per cent of the time, if your stud's color potent."

"How popular are Appaloosas?" I asked our sun-bronzed friend.

"They're the coming breed!" he cried confidently. "Another few years and they'll be outselling Quarter Horses. Good spotted yearling brings as much as three thousand dollars right now, if the line's right."

"What do you mean, 'if the line's right?' " asked Frank. "I thought you said you could breed to common mares?"

"You can. I mean the stud should be registered and out of Thoroughbred or Quarter Horse stock."

I never mastered the old math so I certainly's don't know how to deal with the new, but three thousand dollars a colt sounded like second helpings of hay all 'round. If we sold four or five colts a year we could put some kind of heating system in the main house. Maybe we could even afford a rug for the den. Some day there might be color television. . . . I returned from my heady, soaring calculations to hear Frank say, "How much does it cost to breed to a good Appaloosa stud?"

"You can breed to any of mine for a hundred and fifty dollars," said the affable Mr. Barstow and he handed Frank his card. "Dollar and a half a day mares' board, figuring thirty-day minimum board so we can be sure the mare's caught. And you pay for a vet check before breeding."

He whipped a battered wallet out of his jeans' pocket and from it selected some color snapshots which he extended to Frank.

"There's my last crop of yearlings out of two studs."

I leaned over for a look at the snapshots.

"Every last one of them. Got the pictures of their mommas color with a flashy spatter of spots across its loins.

"Oh, how cute they are!" I cried.

"You get those out of solid color mares?" asked Frank.

"Every last one of them. Got the pictures of their mommas to prove it!"

"And were you able to sell them all for a good price?" I asked.

"Sold them for enough to buy a fifteen-hundred acre spread up north in Idaho and that's where I'm heading soon as I sell my next crop," said Mr. Barstow.

"Here." He thrust a book at me. He'd been carrying it under his arm along with a whole wad of show entry papers. "This here book gives the history of the Appaloosa horse. Got it from the Appaloosa Horse Club. Whyn't you read up on 'em. You can have it with my compliments. When you're ready to go in the Appaloosa business, just you hustle your mares over to my place. Shows you how to get to it right on my card. I guarantee loud color colts every time . . . if you want to pay a hundred dollars extra at time of breeding for the guarantee. That'll entitle you to a second breeding at half price case you don't get spots the first time."

This last was rolled out all in one breath without sufficient pauses for me to tell whether he was offering a genuine bargain or not.

He slid off the fence, tilted his Stetson low over his brow and disappeared in the throng of breeders.

"Frank!" I cried excitedly, as soon as he was out of ear shot. "Let's go in the Appaloosa business. Anyone would love a little colt with loud spots like that on its rump. They're so cute. They look just as if they sat in a bucket of paint. I'm convinced Mr. Barstow is right. Appaloosas will be the coming breed. Who could resist them? And you don't need registered mares, that means we could afford to raise them. A hundred and fifty dollars is cheap for a breeding if you can sell a colt for three thousand dollars . . . "

Frank dragged me, still yapping, away from the show ring, shoved me into the Camino and headed for the Bar None.

That night when he was seated in the kitchen with his feet tilted ceiling-ward and his pipe sending up signals of content-ment, I read to him from the book that Chuck Barstow gave us:

"Twenty-four centuries ago there appeared in the pages of history a remarkable breed of spotted horses, famed for intelli-gence, speed and endurance. Revered in Ancient Persia as the sacred horses of Nisaea, and in China as the heavenly horses of Emperor Wu Ti, these beautiful animals have again come into their own, through the intelligent breeding program of the Nez Perce Indians and the organized efforts of western stockmen."

I looked through the walls of our kitchen to behold the parched, grassless pastures of the Bar None, covered with a sea of loud colored Appaloosas. There were spotted colts every-where. And, as the colts were sold, there was money every-where. Money for all the things we'd been dreaming of . . .

"Frank! We've got to start raising Appaloosas. No one could resist a horse so colorful, so romantic, so heavenly . . . "

Silence, save for the sound of teeth gritting on pipe stem.

"Frank, please. It would be such fun to raise those adorable little colts with the spotted rumps. And if they really sell for that much . . . "

Sound as of pipe stem feeding through meat grinder.

"Frank . . . please?"

Slowly Frank removed the pipe from his mouth.

"We'll breed one mare to an Appaloosa, Cindy, And we'll see what we get. If we get a spotted colt we'll see what kind of money it brings. If it brings real money we may become Appaloosa breeders."

I looked at him in astonishment.

"Why you sly fox! You're just as hooked on those cute little spotted rumps as I am!"

"They are pretty to look at," said Frank, smiling a glazed smile.

We sat there in the kitchen for a long time with spots dancing before our eyes.

Frank bred Cindy to one of Chuck Barstow's part-Thoroughbred Appaloosa studs and we had eleven months to wait to see if her colt turned out to be spotted. In the interim I boned up on Appaloosas in the book Chuck Barstow so wisely gave us. Every evening I'd regale Frank with some new bit of fascinating information regarding the breed.

"Frank, did you know that there are two kinds of Appaloosas? Blanket and Leopard."

"What's the difference?"

"Well, the blanket has spots across the rump or all the way up its back to the shoulders. But a leopard has spots all over its body."

"I think I'd like the blanket best. The other might look just like a spotted horse."

Next night I had an additional revelation to share with Frank.

"It says here in order to be eligible for registration a genuine Appaloosa must have skin mottlings around its eye, nose, and sex organs; its hoofs must have vertical black and white stripes and it must have white around its eye like a human eye. No other horse has that kind of eye. Isn't that interesting?"

"Very." This muttered around his pipe.

"And a true Appaloosa has a very thin mane and tail. That's another breed characteristic."

Following night.

"Frank."

"Hm-hm."

"According to this book it isn't so easy to get a colt with spots. Not as easy as Mr. Barstow said. There's all sorts of combinations that will kill your color."

"Like what, for instance?"

"Well you can't breed to a Palomino, or a Tennessee Walking Horse Roan, or a paint, or a grey or a dun-colored horse or a horse with blue eyes. Any one of those backgrounds works against the Appaloosa spotting."

"What works with it?"

"They don't seem to know."

Silence punctuated by pipe puffing.

"Frank."

"Hm-hm."

"Do you think Cindy will have a spotted colt?"

"Why don't you ask Cindy?"

Further on in the Appaloosa book I read that the Indians, when they were breeding for Appaloosas, sometimes helped mother nature along by applying a little "good medicine" to the mare during her gestation period. They would mix up a colored concoction and dip their fingers in it and press their hand print on the mare's rump, hoping thus to exert a strong prenatal influence toward rump spots.

As I stared long and hard at Cindy during the long months of her in-waiting period, I found it increasingly difficult to resist the temptation to try a little "good medicine" of my own.

As the time for spring foaling drew near, Frank developed the rather grim and harried expression I know means he needs some ranch help.

"Let's try for day help this time," I suggested.

"Who's going to go back and forth from this place?" he answered.

"I'll call the state employment office and see if they know of anyone. If they have their own car or live not too far away, it might be a possibility."

The ever-hopeful state employment man responded to the cry for help by sending us Lupe, a dark-eyed, handsome young Mexican gentleman who arrived at the Bar None in a Buick Century painted canary yellow.

Lupe lived about twenty miles from the ranch and didn't mind driving back and forth to work. It seemed he planned to marry soon and the Buick belonged to his intended, Rosita.

Lupe brought Rosita to meet us. She was a woman about forty, almost twice Lupe's age, broad of beam and round of face and, surprisingly enough, she spoke excellent English. Rosita was surrounded by a clutch of cackling children, from toddlers to teen-agers, the offspring of previous marriages.

All of the youngsters had flashing black eyes, glistening white teeth, and gleaming black hair.

Lupe drew me aside while Rosita took the children on a tour of the ranch.

"You have lots of furniture in barn, si?" he asked eagerly.

"Si."

"Rosita and me we need furniture to get married. I work for it, si?"

"I think you'd better ask Mr. Griffith," I said hesitantly.

Lupe continued to wheedle but I wasn't listening. I glanced toward the pasture and the sight I saw sent my stomach on an upswing that collided with my plummeting heart. Three of Rosita's muchachos were attempting to mount an unbroken yearling; a fourth was about to crawl under a corral fence and into the yard with one of our young studs. Several were chasing Gloria and Granville, the guineas; one was dragging Slinky, my pet cat, by the tail and another was about to shinny up a eucalyptus tree.

"Lupe!" I gasped, interrupting his fervent exhortation, "the children! They'll be killed. Please! Get them back in the car!"

Rosita, hearing my cry, gave a command in Spanish and instantly her offspring fell into line behind her as she rolled toward the car.

"What in H is going on out here?" cried Frank as he crawled out from under a tractor to see what was causing all the commotion.

"It's just Lupe and his bride-to-be," I answered quickly. "Lupe's figured out a way to save you lots of money."

Frank flashed his Doubting Thomas look at me.

"Lupe's willing to work for furniture instead of wages," I explained.

"Furniture's worth money, isn't it?" snapped Frank. "Where's the saving?"

"Well . . . we really don't need that old furniture," I said lamely. "If it sits in the barn much longer the mice will eat it up. Lupe and Rosita need it a lot more than we do. They can't even get married without it . . ."

Frank gave a snort and disappeared under the tractor again.

Lupe knew when not to press an advantage.

"I'll be by mañana for the furniture," he said, sotto voce. He and his ready-made family piled into the Buick; hair, teeth and eyes all sending forth a bright scintillation.

Next evening Lupe had the good fortune to come by when Frank was away from the ranch inspecting a neighbor's new foal. Optimistically Lupe brought with him a huge open bed truck, and two of Rosita's older huskier teen-agers.

"We load the furniture now, Mrs. Griffith, si?" he asked.

"Oh, Lupe, I really think Mr. Griffith should be here when you load it," I began uncertainly. Just then Frank pulled up alongside Lupe's truck in the El Camino, and I beat a hasty retreat.

As I ran toward the house I could hear the sounds of a scrambled altercation. Sentences began in English and ended in Spanish. Others began and ended with cuss words.

After a while I saw the truck move down the lane loaded with a television set, several chairs, a table, a refrigerator—there were several other items that I couldn't make out distinctly, but at least Lupe and Rosita would be able to set up housekeeping.

"You were sweet to let Lupe have the furniture," I said to Frank later. We were seated at the kitchen table going over breeding records and making a note of worming dates, hoof trimmings and the number of times the older horses had had their teeth floated.

The roar escaping from the other side of the table caused me to drop my pencil.

"I didn't let Lupe 'have' anything! He's to pay for that furniture out of his wages. A hundred and seventy-five dollars!"

I dove under the table for my pencil, deciding not to make any comment.

Lupe proved to be a less than diligent ranch hand.

He let the water overflow when he watered the stock; forgot to lock the gates when he turned the mares out to pasture; left grooming aids where we could fall over them and managed to hide all the tie ropes.

Brought to task by Frank, Lupe lowered his thick, curling lashes and said: "A man who is about to become a husband cannot always keep his thought on his work."

When he received his second pay check Lupe left the Bar None never to return.

The man at the state employment agency who knew Lupe, told us Rosita disappeared the very day Lupe had planned to marry her. Rosita took the furniture with her.

I held a twitch on a mare while Frank trimmed her fetlocks.

"Do you hear what I hear?" I asked.

We listened.

"Sounds like a horse," said Frank. "A very slow horse."

Just then a donkey appeared in our lane. A man and woman straddled it tandem.

And that's how Quintas and Maria came into our lives.

Since the state employment man informed us that he hadn't one derelict willing to accept a ranch job, we managed the chores alone after Lupe's departure. But the work was getting out of hand and Frank and I were getting grumpity, so when Quintas asked if we could use a couple of steady workers Frank leaped to the bait.

Quintas and Maria were hired with the understanding that Quintas would do the outside work and Maria would help me indoors.

But things didn't work out that way.

Quintas was a full-blooded Yaqui Indian: a square little block of a man, with dark skin, diamond-bright eyes, and an up-curling grin that I found very appealing.

As soon as he decided that they were both hired, Quintas dragged a threadbare blanket off the donkey and swung it, hammock-fashion, between two trees, then stretched out in it.

There he remained during the heat of the day, dreaming and dozing, and occasionally rousing himself sufficiently to berate Maria if she seemed to be lagging behind in her work.

Maria was a good looking woman, much younger than Quintas, who spoke perfect English and gave the appearance of being a person of refinement—until she opened her mouth. She had absolutely no teeth!

"How did you happen to marry Quintas?" I asked her one day. "You are not Indian, are you?"

"No," she answered in her low, sad voice. "I am American. I was born in Los Angeles. Quintas brought the vegetables from my uncle's farm in Oxnard to the market where I worked. He got me pregnant. I was only fourteen when our first boy was born. There were four other boys. They are all grown now and in jail."

From the tone of Maria's voice you would have imagined that after much striving her four sons had finally made Harvard.

"Woman, you talk too much," growled Quintas, from his

lookout post beneath the live oak trees. "Go now and tend to your work!"

Maria not only fed and watered the livestock, mucked out the stalls and gathered the eggs; she also kept the house spotlessly clean.

Quintas not only found fault with everything she did, he also offered helpful criticism regarding the management of the ranch.

"You feed your horses too much," he told Frank frequently. "Those who waste will some day want. Old Indian saying."

When customers appeared Quintas assumed the role of genial host, entered into lively conversation with them, and just as Frank was about to consummate a sale he would make an acid remark concerning the quality of our livestock.

Frank was mounted on one of our older geldings, putting it through its paces before a prospective buyer, when Quintas spoke up.

"If my ancestors had a horse like that they would feed it to the goats," he said.

"Those people had no intention of buying that horse anyway," I told Frank later when he exploded with a violence that rocked the rafters. "Anyway, they just thought Quintas was being funny."

"Quintas is about as funny as a horse with two broken legs," snarled Frank. "And he isn't going to be around here after pay day."

But Frank's wrath melted whenever he saw Maria going docilely about her chores. And though he threatened to cut Quintas's hammock out from under him and then continue cutting, Quintas and Maria stayed on.

I rather liked having a woman around the ranch after being without feminine companionship for so long, and Maria was really an excellent housekeeper.

"Maria has such a pretty face, she'd be beautiful if she had dentures," I said to Frank one evening over a game of Chinese Checkers.

"Quintas would knock them down her throat. Then make her cough them up so he could hock them," said Frank.

It seemed best to change the subject.

But I kept imagining what Maria would look like with beautiful flashing teeth. She could get away from Quintas, the ruffian, and get a decent job!

"Maria," I asked her next day as we chopped onions for the enchiladas, "Have you ever thought about getting dental plates?"

"Many times," she said sadly. "But I have no money. Whatever I make Quintas takes."

"Have you any idea what plates would cost?"

"Two hundred and sixty dollars!" she replied so promptly that I stared at her in astonishment.

"I have already asked a dentist and so I know," she said by way of explanation.

"I will loan you the money for your dentures, Maria," I said on impulse. "You can clean for me and pay it back."

Tears streamed from Maria's lustrous dark eyes. She seized my hands and covered them with kisses until I felt miserably embarrassed.

"You must not mention our bargain to Quintas or to my husband," I warned her.

"Never! I swear!" She raised her right hand to the sky.

"I'll make the check payable to the dentist," I said, thinking this was a crafty way to keep Quintas from squandering the money on himself.

"Good," said Maria. "That is the only way."

She went through a series of dental fittings and a short time later said the dentist demanded payment. I gave her a check for two hundred and sixty dollars, made out to the dentist, and the following week Maria dazzled us all with her flashing store teeth.

She looked twenty years younger and carried herself with new confidence.

Frank saw the check entry when he went over the bank statement. He tracked me down at once, breathing fire.

"It's only a loan. Maria will pay it back working for us," I said blithely, not daring to look at him.

"You are hopeless!" he cried when he could talk. "You will die in the poor house and be buried in Potter's Field."

"And you'll be there next to me," I retorted. "I know what you do when the ranch hands corner you with a sob story. You give them a handout. Only you're sneaky about it."

Frank stomped back to his bookkeeping, trailing a blue cloud of cuss words and pipe smoke behind him.

For the remainder of the week Maria worked tirelessly. After she finished the ranch chores she washed windows; laundered the curtains; cleaned the range and the refrigerator; polished the furniture; put new shelf paper in all the closets and aired the rugs and blankets.

Saturday night as she and Quintas rode off into the sunset on Pobrecito, the donkey, she waved to me until they were no more than a blur on the horizon.

It was the last time we saw either one of them.

Several months later the man at the state employment office told us that Maria got a job in a small parts factory.

"Is she still living with Quintas?" I asked, hoping the dentures had accomplished their purpose and set Maria free.

"Oh, yes! Her boss says Quintas calls for Maria every pay day and she always gives him her check."

The dust from the state employment man's car had scarcely settled in the lane before Frank cried: "Well?"

I burst out laughing.

"So you're right again! Just as you were with the roosters. What does it prove except that you're smarter than me?"

Quintas and Maria were long forgotten. We were help-less once more and enjoying it. Life had settled into a peaceful routine at the ranch.

I was scrubbing out a watering trough, ploughing the steel brush through a week's accumulation of green, spongy, algae, when I heard Frank wahooing and hollering from the pasture.

There could only be one reason for such exuberance. Cindy must have delivered her foal.

I dropped brush and hose and hurled myself through the pasture gate to meet him head on!

We staggered, recovered and sprinted for the foaling area. There stood Cindy, slim, trim and perfectly composed, and, at her side, nuzzling her tummy in his search for breakfast, stood a perfectly conformed little chestnut stud colt WITH A SPOTTED RUMP!

Cindy had produced our first Appaloosa!

We were Appaloosa breeders!

We were in the Appaloosa business!

We joined the Appaloosa Horse Club, put Appaloosa Breeder stickers on both doors of the El Camino, and hung an Appaloosa Emblem on the gate of the Bar None.

We named our little Appy "Lollapalooza"—"Lolly" for short —and later he became quite famous when his dad, Cojo Rojo, starred in the Universal Picture, "The Appaloosa," with Marlon Brando.

As quickly as possible we bred six of our solid color mares to loud-colored permanently registered Appaloosa stallions.

The following spring we got ready to reap our harvest: A sea of spotted colts that would convert to a jeep load of cash.

Queenie, a bay Morgan mare, was due to foal first, and, within a few days of her foaling date, a young boy who introduced himself as Bill Douglas appeared at the ranch. Bill said he was majoring in film at college and he asked permission to take some stills of ranch life, since that was one of his class assignments.

"Frank!"

Frank knew instantly from the excited tone of my voice that I was about to leap off the deep end again and he stood waiting for the splash.

"What is it this time?"

"Bill can take a picture of Queenie having her colt! It will be the first movie of the birth of an Appaloosa. He may be able to sell it to the Appaloosa Horse Club or Disney; he'll get rich and we'll get famous."

"Have you worked with a movie camera?" Frank asked Bill.

"Not too often. But I can sure try," said Bill. He was a sweet boy, quiet and serious of mien. He had curly brown hair and rather soulful brown eyes, with something of a colt's trustingness about them. "I never saw any animals born. I've lived in the city all my life," he said a little uncertainly. "Do you think if I watched this horse get born it might make me throw up?"

"Oh, Bill, never!" I hastened to reassure him. "The birth of a foal is beautiful to see. It all happens so quickly and neatly. You'll be thrilled by it."

Bill still looked doubtful.

"Maybe if I could spend some time at the Bar None getting to know the animals I could get used to the idea," he said hesitantly.

"That's just what you should do!" I cried eagerly. "You can stay in the help's cottage. There's no one in it now."

Bill returned the next day with a carload of camera equipment including the most elaborate movie camera I'd ever seen, photofloods, juice boosters, light meters, endless packs of film and a stack of books on photography.

He followed us around the ranch with the movie camera, taking shots of anything that crossed his path.

"Bill certainly doesn't mind using up film," I said to Frank. "Just think of all the publicity we'll get when Bill gets a picture of the birth of an Appaloosa on film."

"I wish he'd stop taking shots of me shoveling manure," Frank muttered. "And asking stupid questions."

"What do you mean stupid questions!"

"Well, when the roosters take after the hens Bill wants to know why they're fighting. He called a gelding a girl horse and —well—I just hope he knows more about photography than he does about animals."

"Now remember, Bill's only an amateur," I reminded Frank.

"But we couldn't afford a professional photographer and it's real sweet of Bill to at least make a try at it. How could he help getting good pictures with all that magnificent equipment. I've never seen a more elaborate movie camera!"

Frank sucked on his pipe and looked thoughtful.

"He said he borrowed the camera and he's just learning how to use it. It belongs to some relative who's a professional cameraman."

"Bill has plenty of time to master that camera before Queenie foals," I said confidently. "You know she isn't due for at least two days."

"Queenie can fool us yet," remarked Frank between pipe puffs.

"Bill says he won't even go to sleep tonight in case she surprises us."

"That might not be a bad idea. I think the old girl's about home."

At dusk that day Bill set up his lights and equipment next to the corral where we'd arranged for Queenie to have her colt. As darkness fell we joined him on the far side of a live oak tree where we could watch Queenie as she paced back and forth, without being seen by her.

Every so often Queenie would switch her tail and bite at her flank.

Frank and I recognized foaling signals.

"I think I'd better turn on the stable lights," said Frank, and he sprinted across the yard.

"Get everything ready," I whispered to Bill. "This is it!"

"Y-you m-mean she's going to have her colt n-now?" gasped Bill.

"Any minute."

The stable lights flashed on as I spoke and I caught a glimpse of Bill's face. It was chalk white and his upper lip was beaded with moisture.

"Are you all right, Bill?" I asked in concern.

"I-I don't know," he said shakily. "I'm afraid I'm going to faint."

"Oh, Bill, you musn't. Not with that expensive camera that doesn't even belong to you!" I cried.

"Rubye! Come quick!"

I turned like a fire horse at Frank's cry, forgetting Bill instantly. Queenie thumped to the earth and her water bag broke. The colt was on its way.

I crawled between the corral rails and Frank and I went into action.

Silently and efficiently, following a system we had worked out after long months of practice, we performed our duties as midwives. At one point in the delivery Queenie seemed to be having trouble and we got down on our hands and knees to give her a hand.

Not once did we think about Bill.

A few minutes of struggle and the foal was out and in the clear, gleaming wetly in the glare of the flood lights. Dimly I could hear the whirr of the movie camera but I paid no attention to it. My thoughts were entirely on Queenie.

"It's a stud!"

"All okay?"

Frank looked Queenie over carefully.

"All okay."

I breathed a sigh of relief and wiped my hands on a gunny sack.

Then I remembered Bill.

I glanced about and saw him stretched out on his stomach, the camera to his eye. It was whirring efficiently.

"Bill! You didn't faint! And you've got a perfect angle there. I'll bet you got everything! A perfect record of the birth of an Appaloosa."

Bill got unsteadily to his feet.

"Is that what a baby Appaloosa looks like?" he asked.

I wheeled to look at the foal.

Queenie still lay on her side but the youngster was staggering erect.

"Frank!" I let out a howl of anguish. "Look at the colt!"

"What! What is it? What's the matter!"

"It hasn't a single spot!"

Frank threw the beam of the ranch lantern on the wobbling baby.

"Well I'll be damned!" he exclaimed. "I was so worried about Queenie I never noticed . . . you're right! No spots!"

The three of us stared at the colt.

"Won't it get spots later?" Bill asked.

"They sometimes do," I began, but Frank interrupted.

"I doubt this one will. It doesn't have an Appaloosa eye or Appaloosa stripes on its hoofs."

"You didn't get the record of an Appaloosa birth after all, Bill."

"It doesn't matter, Mrs. Griffith. I did get a colt being born. I'll get the best grade in my class! Gee I'm glad I know Appaloosa Breeders like you . . ."

The Appaloosa Breeders were breeders in name only.

Our mares produced five more colts within the next two months.

Here's how the spots talleyed at the end of the season:

Queenie, Bay Mare, bred to loud-colored, permanent registered Appaloosa stud, produced a solid bay colt WITHOUT SPOTS.

Big Mama, Liver Colored Chestnut Mare, bred to loud-colored, permanent registered Appaloosa stud, produced Christine. (Need we say more?)

Tammy, solid color brown mare, bred to loud-colored, permanent registered Appaloosa stud, produced a black colt with one white point AND NO SPOTS.

Missy, solid color Chestnut Mare, bred to loud-colored, permanent registered Appaloosa stud, produced a solid color chestnut filly that developed tiny white snowflake spots as a two-year-old.

Cindy, solid-color brown mare, bred back to loud-colored, permanent registered Appaloosa stud, produced a Palomino colt the following spring. (Horsemen said that this couldn't be done, but Cindy did it!)

We thought this pitiable paucity of spots might be due to the fact that we bred grade mares to Appaloosa studs. But several of our friends who are Appaloosa Breeders, with far more cash and experience than we have, bred permanent registered, loud-colored Appaloosa mares to permanent registered loud-colored Appaloosa studs and got NO SPOTS.

The Appaloosa color inheritance patterns are mysterious. Color prepotent Appaloosa studs—so-called because they have a record of producing loud colored colts on an eighty-to-ninety per cent average when they are bred to solid-color mares, sometimes upset the averages inexplicably and produce only fifty per cent colored colts.

Since only loud-color foals bring good prices, a fifty per cent color average can cut your profits in half.

We had learned a lot about Appaloosa breeding since the night of Queenie's delivery. And we learned a lot about amateur photographers, too.

We waited with poorly restrained eagerness for Bill to return with his film record of the birth of an Appaloosa (that didn't Appaloose); but it was weeks before he finally drove in; made a tour of the ranch; greeted all the horses and exclaimed over Queenie's foal—named Wilhem, in his honor.

When the final pleasantry had been exchanged and he still made no reference to the pictures, I could stand it no longer and burst out:

"Bill! What did you get on your movie camera of Queenie's delivery? Did you really get the whole story on film?"

Bill was silent for several seconds; then he spoke rather timorously.

"I sure hate to tell you this, Mrs. Griffith," he began, then stopped.

I knew without his telling me.

"You ran out of film! Is that it, Bill?"

"Right after about three feet of film, yes."

I looked at Bill and I felt so sorry for him I was unable to speak.

"But I sure got some wonderful shots of you and Mr. Griffith shoveling manure," he said brightly.

Well—there's more than one way to make a movie debut. Earthiness is what counts in movies these days—who knows, we may turn out to be stars!

7

Miami Jackson — A Lonesome
Gal's Pals

Miami Jackson, a long, lithe, dynamic Negress, tall as a
Watusi and greatly resembling one (in the manner of her
hair-do, an upstanding crew cut, and the looseness of her stride
—she could cover as much territory in one reach as a Tennessee
Walking Horse) came to the Bar None through the courtesy
of Herkimer Beane, a Negro Employment Broker.

Replying to Mr. Beane's dignified ad in the Los Angeles
Times, with its glowing references to reliable ranch help, we
happened to mention that we might be able to use a reliable
housekeeper.

Within seconds Mr. Beane had pinpointed our location on a
Freeway Systems Map that he kept handy on his office wall,
and a few hours later he appeared at the ranch in an irridescent
purple Lincoln, along with Miami.

As Miami unfolded her long frame from the Lincoln and
rose to her full height, any horseman would have agreed: she
stood eighteen hands high at the withers.

We expected Mr. Beane to extoll her virtues or at least to
give us some idea of her background and experience, but he

completely ignored Miami and tried most earnestly to sell himself to Frank as a potential ranch foreman. When this failed he said that he knew how to muck stalls and exercise horses, having worked for years at the track.

Herkimer Beane followed Frank around the ranch for at least an hour, pointing out that he was a country boy who longed to return to the soil. But when he became convinced that Frank had no intention of hiring him, he jumped in the purple Lincoln and drove away without so much as saying farewell to Miami. And, as he disappeared down the lane, it became apparent to us that we had hired her.

We imagined that Miami Jackson had been born in Florida. But, as it turned out, she came from Memphis, Tennessee. And, she explained tearfully, she had no friends at all in Los Angeles: only a sister and brother-in-law, whose home was over-crowded, which is why they had turned her out.

Miami was so tall, and I so short, that I had to bend my head backward every time I addressed her. Also, she was so thin and angular that she seemed to be traveling in several directions at once. Her elbows went one way, her shoulder blades another, and her knees got lost on the way.

"Do you think we should give her a try?" I asked Frank, timorously. I was really very humble after our experience with the little princesses.

"We don't seem to have much choice," said Frank gruffly. "Keep her a week and see how you make out."

Miami, who preferred to be called Amy, because she didn't like her name, proved to be one of those rare gifts to humanity: a tireless, dynamic, whizz of a house cleaner.

Miami had a positive grudge against dirt and refused to tolerate it in any form. She despised dirt with such thoroughness that she dedicated her life to pursuing it, attacking it, destroying it, and then pursuing it again. And not just surface dirt. Miami cleaned anything and every thing. She cleaned like a dark tornado. And when she cleaned she tore the whole house apart and she did everything the hard way.

It was like watching a gigantic, swooping black bird in action to see her sail through the house—arms flailing, legs following, full of sound and fury, lifting sofas as if they were pillows, and moving gigantic chests and huge sideboards as if they were matchboxes.

When Miami finished her cleaning, the house sparkled. The only trouble was she was never satisfied with the results of her labor. The following day she cleaned house again.

She used prodigious quantities of cleaning aids: water softeners, vinegar, floor wax, bowl cleaner—they all disappeared as if they were poured down a bottomless pit.

When Miami cleaned the floors she first removed the old wax: a tortuous ear-shattering process that raised clouds of dust. This took hours. Then she'd wash the floors; dry them; pour on fresh wax and polish it till you couldn't take a step without sliding for home. Every piece of furniture was reflected in a radiant pool. This took several more hours.

When the floors resembled a skating rink, Miami would tackle the windows. Huffing and puffing at them, and painstakingly scraping off fly specks with a splayed brown thumb, she'd worry them till they did what they say windows do in the Windex commercials: they disappeared.

Never had we lived in such immaculate surroundings. And never had we felt less relaxed or more miserable, for Miami would watch us with her bird-bright eyes and if we tracked dust in from outdoors or dirtied an ash tray or left a finger mark on a piece of gleaming furniture, she would fall-to-emptying, scrubbing, or polishing—her black brows lowering over her broad nose like storm clouds.

When we paid Miami her first week's salary she produced a contract from Herkimer Beane that stated she must send him the entire amount. She had signed it and it looked legal so we sent the money to him for her.

At the end of three weeks of Miami's constant, tyrannical cleaning I got her stopped long enough to have a chat with her. It wasn't easy to talk to Miami. She would never light long enough for you to get more than a sentence out. And if she did poise on the edge of a chair she always looked ready for flight—as if even the slightest arm movement would send her skittering off into space.

As gently as possible I told her how pleased we were with her house cleaning but we wished she would relax once in a while and not clean all the time.

"Couldn't you just sit down now and then and take it easy, Miami?" I asked her.

I was totally unprepared for the disastrous reaction that followed. Miami's whole gaunt body seemed to fly apart; the face cracked up; sobs shook the angular frame with an intensity that caused the chair she sat on to rattle. Tears cascaded down her brown cheeks; her mouth drew back from her white flange of teeth; and a thin, keening howl emerged from her pipestem of a throat.

I was horrified but it would have been useless to say anything. This was emotion that had to spend itself; an agony of inner turmoil pent up too long. Eventually Miami gained sufficient control to gasp through her sobs:

"I clean all the time on account of when I don't clean I gets lonesome!"

The last word rocketed into a shrieking wail. This was the crux of the matter. This the sore anguish that over-wound and over-drove Miami's too high-powered motor and threatened to plummet her clear off the track.

My horror gave way to pity which was replaced by shame.

To think that we never suspected the craving of this poor creature for affection and attention; for the sight of faces like her own; the sound of voices keyed like hers; for mutual interests and shared confidences; for friendship's sweet antidote to her raw, corrosive loneliness.

I patted her bony shoulder and we made a pact. I would get in touch with her sister and brother-in-law and arrange for them to visit her on weekends and bring some friends with them. Miami would never be lonesome again. And, with her loneliness assuaged, she might become not just a frenetic cleaner but a normally efficient cleaner. The prospect seemed happy for both of us.

Miami's sister, who was tall as she, and her brother-in-law, who was pint sized and quite rotund, arrived the next weekend in a woody station wagon loaded with family and friends. Besides two sets of twins, aged three and four (not identical), who were the children of Miami's sister, there were four or five teen-agers; and I realized with a shock that for all her vast height and seeming maturity Miami herself was just a child: only seventeen as it turned out.

One youth, no more than seventeen himself, followed Miami around with a fatuousness that could only imply amorous intentions. This proved to be Devaleen Bainbridge, whom she introduced as her boyfriend.

Devaleen brought with him Miami's most treasured possession, a beat-up but still workable portable stereo record player. And at least three hundred records.

The transformation that took place in Miami when the first record sent out its rock 'n' roll rhythms was so phenomenal we couldn't believe it even as we beheld it. She clasped her rawboned hands; extended her bony elbows and began to rotate her hips in a paroxysm of ecstasy. Her eyeballs rolled skyward, leaving only glaring orbs of white visible in her black face. Her lips drew back in a lascivious grin and as she began to twist and writhe in sinuous undulations; Devaleen, first, and then the others joined her in an orgy of caterwauling and twisting.

Now on Sundays customers frequently come to the ranch to look at the horses and we were expecting several that day. What would they think if they saw the lawn area in front of the ranch house alive with rocking and rolling Negro visitors, all wailing at the top of their lungs and convulsed in the throes of the Monkey, the Frug, and the Jerk? (Even the two sets of twins were twisting, screaming and shoving at each other, falling down and getting up again, flaunting their little bottoms in an abandoned imitation of their elders.)

Frank and I went indoors, hoping to avoid the astonished looks of any prospective horse buyers who might drive by. We had a hurried consultation. It wouldn't be right to dampen Miami's spirits; they'd been damp too long. Maybe after the first fine flush of ecstatic release wore off we could coax the frenzied dancers inside. We have a large room that's reserved for parties and square dances. Perhaps if we lured Miami's pals in there they could enjoy themselves without attracting too much attention.

As things stood now our front lawn looked like the scene of a Negro revival meeting.

"You must tell Miami that she can't have company in droves," said Frank. "No more than two at a time. And she must entertain them indoors!"

I nodded and peered out the window. The writhings and wrigglings were gaining momentum.

Some people in a station wagon drove in our lane, apparently to have a look at the horses. Seeing Miami and her coterie gyrating wildly, they made a loop around the front lawn and squeaked their tires pulling away.

Frank and I busied ourselves around the ranch, tending to chores and trying to ignore the increasing hullabaloo from the front lawn.

"We really should serve Miami's guests something," I said at last. "They must be frightfully thirsty."

Frank gave me a blistering look that made me feel like a flake of fallout.

"Do you think that's a good way to discourage this sort of thing?" he demanded.

"We shouldn't be rude. They are Miami's friends. Besides, a nice cool drink might take their minds off their dancing."

I fixed ice tea, milk, and cookies for the dancers. But when

I called Miami to ask her to serve them, she didn't hear me. She was stomping both feet, snapping her fingers and bobbing her head in time to the music. Perspiration skidded down her brown face; her hair undulated in an agitation of its own; her eyes were closed; her mouth was pursed in a full-lipped pucker.

Her sister, spying the refreshments, disengaged herself from the pulsating mob and offered to dispense them.

The spell was broken. Dancers dropped exhausted to the ground. Within an hour they took off, promising a return engagement the following weekend.

Long after the last guest had departed, the music continued to thump and beat and Miami sat crouched next to the record player, a vacuous smile on her face; one splayed foot tapping to the rhythm.

I went to bed, slept fitfully, and at two o'clock awoke to hear the record player still wailing. I followed the sound to the front room where I found Miami slumped on the floor sound asleep. I turned off the record player, prodded her awake and managed to guide her to her bed.

Music unwound a too-taut spring in Miami. No longer was she a compulsive cleaner. Moving about in a somnabulistic daze, she would polish the same piece of furniture over and over again, the record player athrob at her side. Eventually Frank and I felt we couldn't listen to one more rock 'n' roll record and we asked her if there weren't something else in her collection she might like to listen to.

Obligingly she switched to spirituals. Their deep, heart-rending cadences pounded through the house from the time Miami got up till she went to bed. Beautiful and meaningful as were the lyrics, they had a depressing effect. How often can you listen to a full-thoated baritone shout accusingly: "Were you there when they crucified my Lord?"

Then, even more accusingly:

"Were you there when they laid him in the tomb!"

I told Miami after four days of this it might be better if she played some rock 'n' roll.

In reply she shut off the record player and lapsed into a morose, sad-eyed silence. This was punctuated occasionally by long, wrenching sighs that bordered closely on moans.

When I found myself beginning to sigh in unison with her I decided it was time for another of our girl-to-girl chats.

"You're not happy, Miami."

"Nom'm"

"Don't you like it here at the ranch? Do you feel you're not being treated properly—is there anything? . . . "

Her face broke into jagged tear-stained pieces and out with a watery sob came the blurted confession:

"I'm lonsesome!"

"Oh Miami, I am sorry. But your friends will be back to-morrow . . ." This was spoken with an inward shudder though with outward equaniminity.

"I ain't lonesome for them. I'm lonesome for my mother!" Her sobs reached an hysterical crescendo.

"Oh poor Miami!" After all she was only a child to be so far from home and confined to a ranch far away from city friends and city amusements.

"Why don't you call your mother tonight when the rates go down, Miami, and have a little talk with her—you do have a phone in Memphis?"

She nodded, unable to speak, but her face was beginning to brighten.

"Talking to your mother for two or three minutes will make you feel a whole lot better. You go ahead and charge the phone call to me."

The next morning Miami had no need of the record player. She sang loud and lustily: "Michael row the boat across, Halle-lulia . . . Michael row the boat across, Haleluliaaaaaaa . . . ."

"Did you have a nice talk with your mother last night, Miami?"

"Oh, yes'm!"

"That's good. You must call her whenever you feel lonely. That way she'll be able to cheer you up before your spirits get too low."

"Yes, ma'am!"

That afternoon Miami's boy friend, his girl friend and another young man drove up in a canary yellow Buick. The car barely made it to the door of the ranch. There it gasped, sputtered and collapsed.

Devaleen leaped out, lifted the hood and clouds of steam rose from the radiator.

"Having car trouble?" asked Frank, bringing a bucket of water with him.

"I reckon we is," said Devaleen brightly. He indicated a ruptured radiator hose. "Needs a new hose and I ain't got the money."

The friends Devaleen had brought with him unloaded a case of records from the trunk of the Buick. They moved toward Miami and I saw them head for the record player.

I drew Frank aside as the thump-thud of the music billowed out of the house.

"We'd better make sure this car will run or they may spend the weekend here," I whispered.

"A new hose could cost seven dollars or more."

"Sounds like a small price to pay for the return of Miami's friends to the city."

"I don't have any here. I'd have to go in town and get one."

"I'll stay here and keep an eye on the place. You go get it."

Cuss words.

"Well do you want them here all weekend?"

More cuss words. But he got in the ranch truck and barrelled out of the driveway.

When he returned the fruggers were still frugging. I had set out once to call them to order but they were having such a good time, their eyes rolled heavenward—their teeth flashing, bodies writhing in an ecstasy of pleasure. I didn't have the heart to poop the party.

When Frank returned we called Devaleen aside and told him we had the hose for his car and Frank offered to help him put it in.

Devaleen looked longingly at Miami, still twisting and writhing. He was obviously very reluctant to tamper with the car; to soil his dress-up clothes; to take time away from his girl. He puttered with the car a few minutes, then assumed the role of a spectator as Frank strained and struggled and finally made the hose connection.

When, at Frank's insistence, he tried to start it up, however, there proved to be more serious trouble.

"We'd better find out what's wrong or you'll never get back to town," said Frank.

When Devaleen saw Frank meant it, and they'd have to work on the car, he stripped off his white satin shirt and skintight black pants and stood in brown khaki Army shorts, ready for anything.

He worked with Frank an hour on the car then pleaded an overwhelming thirst and disappeared indoors. He did not return and when I peered in the window I saw him twisting with the others, his brown chest glistening above the Army trunks.

Frank had become so absorbed in the car he failed to note the passage of time and hadn't realized he was working alone. Two hours later he put the last part back in place, just as Devaleen, neatly dressed, rejoined him.

Devaleen tried the engine and it worked.

As it roared and sputtered his friends climbed in back and Miami appeared, in city clothes, carrying her suitcase.

"Are you going away, Miami?" I asked her.

"I'm going home is where I'm going," she said with a broad smile.

"Home . . . ?"

"To Memphis. That's where. When I talked to mother last night she told me, come home, Miami. Mother married last year and she's expecting. She says she needs me."

Frank and I looked at each other. He was covered with car grease, his clothes crumpled and soiled. He rubbed one arm against the smudge on his cheek but said nothing.

I also remained silent, not knowing whether to express anger or relief.

"It's sure been nice working for you," Miami murmured, looking down at me from her vast height. She collapsed in the Buick like a carpenter's rule angles of knees, elbows, and shoulders all folded into a heap on the front seat.

"Goodbye, Miami," I called weakly.

"Goodbye," her friends called in unison. Each dark face was bisected by a big toothy grin.

As the Buick coughed its way down the lane I walked slowly toward the house, not wishing to tangle with Frank.

Neither of us referred to Miami again . . .

Till the phone bill came in. The calls that Miami had made to her mother in Memphis amounted to thirty-two dollars and eighty-three cents.

"I'll pawn my typewriter and pay the bill," I told Frank, laughing in spite of myself.

"What in H are you laughing at!" he demanded.

"Myself. I have a right to laugh at myself. I'm laughing because I was the one who begged Miami to call her old sainted mother."

"There's no help for you," said Frank gloomily.

"There's no help for either one of us—I hope," I corrected. "Let's not have any help for a while. Please? Not even if help comes to us. Please?"

"Well will you listen to that!" Frank snorted. "You'll be look-ing at the Situations Wanted or calling the state employment office as soon as my back's turned!"

I reached in my pocket and pulled out two ear plugs. I had bought them right after Miami switched to spirituals.

I put them in my ears and set out to mix the grain for the colts.

With the ear plugs I could scarcely make out the familiar cuss words.

8

Gloria and Granville,
the Inseparables

One day Frank began reminiscing about his childhood on a farm in Maryland. He became especially nostalgic in recalling the Guinea fowl they had raised there.

"Crazy critters," he said. "Always in a hurry. Always chasing some invisible bug. Always yelling 'Buckwheat, buckwheat, buckwheat.' And when somebody strange comes on the place all hell breaks loose. They make a clatter you can hear for miles."

He stopped, realizing that he'd made a mistake. As I listened to his tales of the guineas my eyes began flashing "must have" signals.

"Why can't we have some guineas at the Bar None?" I asked him.

He looked dubious.

"Because if you start with a pair of anything you always wind up with a Noah's Ark. You remember what happened when we lived in Connecticut."

I remembered only too well. When we sold out and moved to California we had a cow and a calf; a cat and four kittens; a whole flock of chickens; two English Setters and their thirteen puppies; four adult rabbits and an uncountable number of baby rabbits; two horses, a Welsh pony and the pony's colt; two huge, honking, mud-slinging geese; and four sloppy, waggle-tailed ducks. Trying to find homes for all of them had worn us to a nubbin. We distributed them among neighbors for miles around. Not only in Connecticut but throughout Westchester County.

Frank remembered this with terror but he has a soft spot in in his heart for guineas, so finally he consented to get a few.

After making several inquiries we learned of a "guinea woman" who lived in the Valley where fowl were being zoned out. (It's the old-new story of Southern California.) So we made a pilgrimage to her poultry farm.

We arrived before dusk of a summer evening to behold a ramshackle house dating from the Valley's Chicken Ranch Era, circa 1925.

The delapidated two-bedroom dwelling reposed on an acre of ground, and on either side similar dwellings bore real estate signs announcing that they were "Potential R-3." This meant the neighborhood was about to go into apartment zoning and so an acre of ground was easily worth at least sixty-five thousand dollars. Obviously the guineas were doomed.

The front yard was a shambles of broken orange crates, bits of twisted wire fencing, shattered flower pots and rotting wood. But when we worked our way through this debris to the rear of the house we realized that actually the front yard was a model of neatness compared to what lay behind the house.

Stretching the full length of the narrow acre were not dozens but hundreds of improvised poultry coops. Each had a water drinker and a tree or log for the occupants to roost on, but these were the only niceties. All the fencing was patched, drooping wearily and sadly in need of repair. Within each coop there was a foot-high accumulation of excreta. And scattered among the assemblage of endless coops were stacks of rotting timber and rotten eggs; half-open feed bags and broken bird cages; layers of feathers and kegs of nails; broken fireplace brick and mouldy straw. All of this was piled in a charming disarray that made it necessary for visitors to clamber over it, under it, around it, and—ugh—through it.

Within the crumbling pens were some of the most amazing representatives of the poultry world I had ever seen. There were white peacocks, blue peacocks, golden pheasants, and ring necked pheasants; lavender guineas and white guineas; quail and partridge, and cornish game hens; banties, barred rocks, minorcas, leghorns, and ancoras.

The inhabitants of this cacophonous jungle were engaged in vociferous vespers, the leit motif of which was supplied by literally hundreds of roosters of every breed, shape, size and color.

At the Bar None we had winced at the prospect of having to live with four roosters; now we found ourselves battered by the crows of four hundred!

Th whole fabric of pulsating sound was threaded with a musk-like odor, so pungent it first assailed then assaulted our nostrils. If asked to define this fullsome odor, I would say that it resembled a refined distillation of carrion and dung and could only have been extracted from an accumulation of at least several decades of poultry droppings.

Our ears were so deafened, our nostrils so outraged, our eyes so agog at this melee we failed to notice the "Guinea Woman" had joined us. She stood silently by, observing our reactions to the bedlam. A slender form and patrician face bespoke the presence of a lady. But the delicacy of the fine-drawn features was misted by tiredness, and the poor woman's skin had a sere, acrid quality that amounted to dessication.

"Do you like my babies?" she asked, and managed to pitch her voice so that it could be heard in spite of the din. "I love every single one of them," she continued, not waiting for a reply. "I feed them 'round the clock. I don't go to bed any more." She sighed. "I just sit in the kitchen in my rocker and doze a few minutes. Then I go out and feed them again. They have to be fed regularly, you know." She fixed her pale, tired eyes on us, apparently hoping to discover if we *really* understood. If we *really* were poultry lovers. "They have to be fed 'round the clock," she repeated. "Right through the night. There are so many of them." She gave a barely perceptible sigh once more, then quickly composed herself.

Remarkably enough she was not untidy. Her rather dispirited, too-long dress was neither soiled nor crumpled but hung on her loosely, as if ready for moulting. Her shoes were men's shoes—splayed, spreading, thickly clotted with poultry manure.

I wondered if she wore them in the house as she sat rocking, between feedings. If she did, I wondered what her kitchen must be like, then quickly decided not to pursue that line of thought.

Further conjecture was halted by an imperious wave of her hand. She beckoned us to follow her. Obediently we fell in line as she lead us to what proved to be the nursery area of her poultry preserve.

The building which we entered had at one time been a greenhouse. Now, stretched its entire length, were row on row of homemade incubators, each with a glaring, fly-specked light bulb dangling above it.

Within the incubators were just-hatched fowl of every description.

There were quail, no bigger than a teaspoon; partridge and pheasant, looking drab and unrecognizeable in their baby plumage; and tossed in every corner, piled under every table, lay mounds of rotting egg shells, tender mementos of little ones who had long since left their babyhood behind them.

The odors outside the nursery had been sufficiently aggressive, but within its confines the stench was that of a battlefield knee-deep in cadavers.

Somehow we managed to wend our way through the reeking tables and putrid rubbish heaps to the back door. We emerged into the darkling night only to find ourselves greeted by a fresh onslaught of sensory impressions.

We were in a back lot completely surrounded by turkeys, ducks, and geese. Apparently these pets were allowed to run loose. And run they did, directly toward us, in a loud, surging swoop! The ducks came first, bills gaping, quacking, and flapping. The turkeys followed, gabbling and hissing and swinging their huge, foot-long wattles, in quivering wrath. Never had I seen anything resembling those wattles! They looked like raw, bleeding masses of peeled brains, or red clustered clods of slashed viscera.

As I backed away from our shrieking attackers in horror, their leader, more wily than the rest, sneaked up behind me and sank his beak in my buttocks. This stratagem drew a pleased smile from our hostess.

"That's Rodney just nipped you," she said in an affectionate tone. "I encourage Rodney to peck at strangers. It keeps children away."

Hastily I slid behind a brush pile out of reach of Rodney.

"Let's get out of here!" I begged Frank. "Pick out some guineas, quick, and let's go!"

Frank was enjoying himself too much to hurry. Since he'd been raised around cantakerous turkeys, he found my terror amusing. But he did manage to convey to the Guinea Woman the idea that we'd like five guinea hens and a rooster.

On hearing this she ushered us back to the guinea pens and now a new facet of her personality revealed itself.

She did not wish to part with any of her charges; not even for money!

As Frank pointed first to this guinea, then that, indicating that he would like to buy it, she would say:

"Oh, I'm sorry! That's Everett. I can't sell Everett. I've had him three years and I'm attached to him."

Frank made a different selection.

"Oh dear no," she cried. "Not Clara. She's just about to set. You can't have Clara!"

It came over me with chill suddeness, as Frank attempted to

do business with the Guinea Woman and she resolutely refused all offers for her "babies," that she was emotionally attached to every single inmate of her fragrant aviary.

Then an even more frightening thought occurred to me!

What if Frank and I should become infected with this same cloying affection for horses!

What if we both became so attached to our precious charges that we refused to part with them?

I visualized stall after stall filled with horses.

Big horses and little horses.

Nursing mares and mares in foal and weanling colts and yearlings and aging horses, overflowing the pastures, ranging on the hills, all fattening at our expense. All producing tons and tons of manure which we had to carry away.

I was appalled at the ghastly prospect. Why even word slinging would be better than pooper-scooping on such a scale!

Listening to the incessant cacklings and gabblings, I was sure I heard derisive laughter. These feathered fiends were laughing at their benefactress! And that's the way the horses would laugh at us!

Somehow Frank managed to persuade our charming hostess to part with six less desirable guineas; five hens and a cock. It wasn't easy. As the soul mother of her little fledglings, she fought Frank all the way.

But no woman can resist Frank when he turns on the Maryland charm.

I should know.

He charmed me right out of my Squirrel Cage.

As we drove home in silence I snuggled up close to Frank in the cab of the Camino and extracted a vow from him.

"Promise me you'll never let us get like the Guinea Woman . . . unable to part with the horses . . . letting them increase and multiply and subdivide and . . . "

He chuckled.

"But I'm serious!" I cried. "You've got to promise me.

Promise you'll always sell a horse the minute you get a buyer
for it."

"I promise."

"Even at a loss?"

"Even at a loss."

I felt better.

Within two weeks the foxes had made off with four of our
guineas. Only two remained; a cock and a hen whom I named
Gloria and Granville.

Possibly it was the shock of seeing their fellow-guineas meet
with untimely ends that caused Gloria and Granville to form
an indissoluble relationship. At any rate they became such a
devoted couple that we always refer to them as Gloria and
Granville, the Inseparables.

Jonathan may have turned out to be a reprobate and a heart-
breaker, but Granville has established a standard of marital
propriety for the whole ranch. He never leaves Gloria's side.
From the time they hop off their roost in the morning till they
hop back at night, you never see one without t'other!

Some wives might find such constant attention emotionally
stultifying.

Not Gloria!

She never tries to slip away to prune her feathers in privacy
or to exchange a little feminine gossip with Winifred or the
hussies.

Apparently Gloria and Granville are like Frank and me;
so satisfied with each other's company that they don't feel the
need of many friendships.

Visitors to the ranch who've never seen guineas frequently
go into shock the first time they meet up with Gloria and her
spouse.

"What are those . . . those things!" guests cry in panic.

"Nature's original pencil-neck geeks," Frank answers.

And the wrestler's term describes them perfectly.

Their tiny, chalk-white heads float above elliptical bodies on thread-thin necks which sprout cilia-like hairs. Their wattles are tiny, cup-like, and brilliant red; and both hen and cock sport little crowning helmets that have a decidedly Mr. John flair. When in motion their legs move so fast they resemble the revolving spokes of a mechanical toy.

The one lovely thing about Gloria and Granville is their plumage. It's a soft, charcoal grey, sprinkled with an overall pattern of tiny white polkadots—nature's own op art. From a distance the dots blend to a muted lavender.

It took me months to discover how to tell the hen from the cock, since they appear to be identical. But I finally noticed that Gloria's wattles lie flat to her head while Granville's pitch forward and look like a little red bow tie tucked under his chin. The government pamphlet on guineas says there's another way to tell the female from the male guinea. The female is the one who makes that delightful rocking-chair sound of "buckwheat, buckwheat." The male doesn't do this.

The pattern of the guineas' day is quite different from that of the chickens. At daybreak they fly out of the trees in which they roost at night and swoop toward the house, making a racket that sounds like a tribe of Watusis turned loose in the underbrush.

The first time I heard the psyche-shattering clatter of the guineas I thought we were the target for an Indian massacre. I ran to the window and saw that the whooping and hollering was coming from Gloria and Granville's pipe-stem necks. I thought they must be in mortal danger but could find no reason for the outburst. Between screechings they pruned their feathers and cocked their heads at the sky; apparently they were simply rejoicing in the languorous warmth of the sun and voicing a heady exuberance while performing their toilette.

As soon as they complete their morning ablutions Gloria and Granville take off on their daily rounds, following a course as circumscribed and preordained as an astronaut's orbit. They wind up their first go-round of the ranch at mid-morning and sit quietly whispering to each other. The sounds that emerge are like little love whistles, muted and meaningful. Then they take a cooperative dust-bath.

First they each make a hollow in the dust and squat down in it, facing tail to tail. Then they flirt their tail feathers, kick the dust out with their hind feet, and send it in flurries over each other's backs. You dust me and I'll dust you, is the way it works out—a remarkable example of conjugal reciprocity.

At least once a year Granville and Gloria attempt to raise a family.

We know when they reach their decision regarding parenthood because we see Granville moping around the ranch by himself, sans Gloria.

The first time I spotted Granville by himself I flew to Frank in a panic.

"Gloria's missing!" I cried.

"Probably nesting," Frank said calmly. "And if she's kooky as most guineas she'll nest in some brush where the foxes will find her."

This thought was heart-piercing!

How would Granville survive without Gloria? Whenever he caught a worm, gurgled a drink from a rain puddle, or dug up our newly planted dichondra, he shared these exciting experiences with Gloria.

If the foxes caught Gloria, Granville would be unable to bear the weight of his grief.

For several days Granville roamed the ranch, forsaken and disconsolate. Then we saw Gloria strolling beside him in the cool of the evening. We thought the worst had occurred and the foxes had made off with her brood, but it turned out that Gloria simply sought a respite from the responsibilities of motherhood on occasion.

Every evening at twilight she would appear to engage in lengthy and thoughtful conversation with her beloved. It was easy to imagine the colloquy.

Granville: "Do you really think we should be kept apart this way, dearest, just so that we can raise children who will undoubtedly desert us as soon as they are grown?"

Gloria: "What if something happened to you, my dear—and there were no little ones to comfort me and to act as a constant reminder of our love?"

Granville: "How like, you, Gloria, to reason so unselfishly. But you know I love you for yourself and I wish you wouldn't make a drudge of yourself for children who most assuredly will never appreciate all you have done for them!"

Whether it was Granville's romantic pleadings or the ferocity of the foxes that ended Gloria's noble sacrifice, we shall never know. But one night we heard a dreadful commotion on the hillside and the next morning Gloria was at Granville's side, minus a patch of feathers and limping.

Apparently the little ones had vanished without a peep before they could pip.

Gloria and Granville followed the same nesting pattern for four years. Each year Gloria gave up the struggle and returned from her nesting place to Granville without a chick.

Like most couples who are childless, Gloria and Granville are self-centered and set in their ways and completely absorbed in each other. I often wonder if Gloria doesn't find Granville's abject devotion somewhat boring. Would she welcome a little indifference? I cannot say. I only know that every night, just as the sun sinks into the arms of night, Granville sings a raucous and ear-splitting love song to Gloria which we refer to as "The Granville Chorus." Though strident and cacophonous, you can tell that it comes from the heart.

Does Gloria appreciate Granville's rapturous outpouring? If she does she seldom reveals the depth of her feelings. While Granville sings she sits and preens her feathers unconcernedly, for all the world like a graceless wife who puts her hair up in curlers while her husband makes violent love to her.

Watching Gloria and Granville I have come to a sad but inescapable conclusion: Gloria takes Granville for granted!

9

Felice,

Whose Joys Proved To Be Boys

During the summer we open the Nick Nack Nook, a little outdoor souvenir stand, and sell Indian jewelry (made in Hong Kong), native rocks, and natural oddities to the few tourists who lose their way in the back country and find themselves trapped in the cul de sac of the Bar None.

Virginia Harley, the cook for a neighboring rancher, knowing that we usually hire a young girl to run the Nick Nack Nook during its busy season, stopped in to see us one day and said she had a niece who would be just right for the job.

Frank and I had recovered from our shattering experience with Miami and could face the possibility of hiring help again. At least, I could. I didn't know about Frank.

"Is it all right if Virginia Harley brings her niece over so we can see if she'd do to run the Nick Nack Nook?" I asked Frank, choosing a time when he had his teeth full of horseshoe nails and almost any reply could pass for an affirmative one.

Frank was resetting one of the mare's shoes and merely nodded.

Virginia Harley brought her niece over the next day.

"This here's Felice," said Virginia Harley, indicating a slender, fragile young girl whose hair had been bleached a pale gold. It was straight and shining and hung to her waist. A forelock of bangs met the upcurling fringe of thickly matted artificial eyelashes that framed deep set eyes of heady, empurpled blue. Felice wore a clinging sheath—a dress with a miniskirt that ended halfway up her thigh; earrings swung to her shoulders; a Cleopatra bracelet gripped her biceps; her lipstick was pale and brightly glistening. This gal was obviously so out she was in and promised to be a terrific drawing card for the Nick Nack Nook.

"That's Felice's little sister, Loralee," added Virginia, and I tore my eyes from the overpowering pulchritude of the job applicant to behold a little red-headed moppet, about five, who peered out from behind the brief miniskirt. Her face was streaked with dirt, her hair touseled, and as she writhed shyly she dug a bare, grimy toe in the dust.

"Say hello to the lady, Loralee." I jumped and looked about me for the source of the harsh and rasping voice. Then I realized it had come from Felice. This lovely creature whose appearance seemed so angelic and dove-like had been blessed with the voice of a crow!

"Come, Loralee. I have a nice cool popsicle for you," I murmured, leading the way to the lawn chairs.

Loralee followed me to the freezer and we returned with popsicles for everyone.

Virginia Harley, who was squat and stolid, with greying hair and a face as seamed as a patchwork quilt, was seated precariously on a straight back chair, not trusting herself to one of the reclining lounges.

Felice was seated in an ancient African campaign chair, the miniskirt considerably minimized.

I excused myself as my guests began licking their popsicles and slipped over to the tack room where I could see Frank, ostensibly polishing tack, but actually enthralled by Felice.

"Do you think we should hire her?" I asked him. "She dresses sort of . . . well . . . "

"Does the half pint go with her?"

"No! That's her little sister, Loralee. Virginia Harley just brought her over to meet us. It's Felice I'm wondering about . . . "

"I think Felice would do nicely in any nook," said Frank.

"Why you're actually smirking!" I cried, looking at him in amazement. Then I took a better look at Felice.

Was I really being smart to . . .

But this was ridiculous.

Felice was probably a darling girl. Just a little . . . eye catching. Exactly what we needed for the Nick Nack Nook.

So Felice became a part of the family.

From the beginning she loved her work. She cleaned and rearranged the jewelry and other bibelots with childish delight. And the customers, especially the male customers, bought rocks and Indian artifacts and any other gewgaw or gimcrack that Felice offered them, without even thinking about the price.

Cow pokes and bronc busters, rodeo riders, ropers, guitar players, and folk singers turned up at the Nick Nack Nook in a steady stream.

And Felice made friends of them all.

They would perch on the corral fence till it was time for Felice to close up shop at the end of the day. Then as the sun slid into the black pocket of the night they'd vie for a chance to take Felice for a stroll.

Felice was very deft at singling out one and making the others wait their turn, but somehow she managed to keep them all happy.

We'd see a different swain each night, heading for the wooded arroyo, an arm around Felice's tiny waist. It was no bigger around than a hand's span; and with her long blonde hair undulating softly behind her, she looked like a sprite or a dryad as she drifted through the dusk.

"One of those young bucks will pop the question to Felice before long," Frank predicted, "and you'll be looking for a new manager of your Nick Nack Nook."

"I'd hate to see her go. I'm rather fond of her," I said and I meant it.

In spite of her flamboyant taste in jewelry, her shattering thigh-high hemlines and her inch-long lashes, there was something very likable about the fair Felice.

Virginia always brought the little moppet, Loralee, to visit Felice at least once a week. Whenever it came time for Loralee to say goodbye, she would cling to Felice and sob and beg Felice to come home with her.

"It's certainly wonderful to see two sisters so attached to each other, isn't it?" I remarked to Virginia Harley as we witnessed a typical, touching departure scene.

She looked at me with her sad bovine eyes but said nothing.

"You're right about Felice," I told Frank. "She's sure to pick a suitor before long. She's been to the picnic grounds with at least ten in the past two weeks. It must be wonderful to be so popular!"

Frank looked at me through his pipe smoke. He said nothing.

"I suppose you can't wait to marry and settle down and have a lovely little daughter like Loralee," I said to Felice next day.

She lifted her thick, matted lashes and looked at me steadily.

"I'm already married, Mrs. Griffith," she said in her jarring, dissonant voice.

"Why, Felice!" It was all I could say. I was overwhelmed at the depth of my naivete. "Is your husband . . . "

"My husband is in Army prison. He went A.W.O.L. because he couldn't bear to be away from me . . . "

That seemed understandable.

Tears spangled the thick, weighted lashes.

"It's so unfair! To keep a husband away from his wife when all he wants is to be with her!"

The following day as Felice and Loralee laughed and exclaimed over some new bracelets that had just arrived at the Nick Nack Nook, I drew Virginia Harley aside.

"Felice told me about her husband," I said, without preamble. "It seems a shame that the Army put him in jail just because he couldn't bear to be away from her . . . "

Virginia Harley looked startled.

"I hate to see Felice unhappy . . . she's been such a good worker . . . and she's so good to her little sister . . ."

Felice placed a bracelet on the little moppet's arm and instantly Loralee threw her arms around Felice and kissed her warmly.

"I've never seen two sisters so devoted," I said.

Mrs. Harley pulled me behind a stack of feed sacks. She spoke in a hoarse, urgent whisper.

"I hate to talk about my own kin, but there's some things you should know. Felice's husband ain't in no jail. Fact is, she ain't got no husband. Loralee ain't Felice's sister, neither. She's her daughter that she had when she was fifteen."

"Fifteen!"

Virginia Harley nodded so violently her jowls quivered.

"Loralee ain't Felice's only kid. She's got two others. By two other husbands . . . that didn't marry her. I knowed I shouldn't of brought Felice here to the Bar None . . . but them people I work for they said I had to get her outta there . . . she'd exhausted all the pokes at our ranch . . . I mean exhausted them!"

"Thanks for straightening me out, Virginia," I said when I could speak. It took the breath out of me to discover I'd fallen for inch-long lashes and spun sugar hair the same as any cowhand! "The season is over for the Nick Nack Nook . . . I hope Felice will be able to find something . . . "

"Oh it's no trouble getting her a job," said Virginia Harley. "That girl'll never be out of employment!"

"You can say that again!" howled Frank later that night when I told him of my talk with Virginia Harley.

"Do you mean to say that you knew all along that Felice . . . " I stopped. He was chuckling and chortling in a way that was really insufferable.

"There she goes heading for the picnic grounds, now, with

the blacksmith," said Frank, pointing out the window. "He's shod every horse and trimmed the colts and I guess he'll start re-shoeing them tomorrow. And to think I could never get a blacksmith out here when I needed one for love or money." The humor of his last words struck him and he lit his pipe and tamped it down with the palm of his hand, still giving off muffled, throaty, extremely offensive chuckles.

When Felice walked into the kitchen at midnight, she found me seated at the kitchen table. Instantly she patted her hair, tugged at her skirt and flicked a curling tongue over her lipstick.

"Felice, you've been a real help at the ranch and we're going to miss you," I said, handing her her pay. "We're closing up the Nick Nack Nook now and your aunt says she'll come for you tomorrow so you'd better have your things ready and packed."

Felice's thick-lashed blue eyes remained expressionless.

"Here's a little parting gift for you, and one for Loralee." I gave her two little rock gem bracelets exactly alike.

At once her face brightened. She gave me a big hug; thanked me profusely in her rough-shod voice and went off to bed humming happily to herself.

Next morning she hopped into the Camino with Frank and waved goodbye gayly, eager for new worlds to conquer.

We imagined we had seen the last of her. But a few months later she reappeared at the Bar None one evening in a shiny black hearse. As we walked hesitantly toward the bizarre conveyance, out jumped a huge man with rich, black shoulder-length hair and a luxuriant thick, curly beard.

The hirsute gentleman stuck out a ham-sized paw, shook hands with Frank, and smiled shyly through his whiskers.

"Gregory Pott, here," he announced. "And I reckon you know my little bride."

Beneath a ledge of bangs, thick lashes fluttered, revealing twin pools of loveliness. It was indeed, Felice.

A wan, worn, Felice, I discovered, on closer examination, as we chatted together.

Dark roots showed at the base of the ashen blonde hair. Her lashes were badly frayed and needed replacing. Her dress was the same in which she had appeared at the Bar None. It was soiled and stretched to the point of bursting. Yes, Felice was expecting.

Gregory Pott, her husband(?), informed us that he had once been a wrestler but left the ring to become a mortician's helper. The mortician's business having declined, Mr. Pott fell heir to his boss's hearse. This proved a fortunate acquisition since Pott had converted the hearse to a camper and he and Felice planned to live in it.

We waved goodbye to Felice and her gargantuan companion and a curl of dust followed them down the lane.

As I walked beside Frank to the stables, I heard the blacksmith who had courted Felice mutter to his apprentice assistant: "Felice ain't so tasty-lookin' as she oncet was. If you ask me I'd say that girl's plumb gone to Pott!"

The laughter of the two men rang out, harsh and metallic as the crack of the sledge on the anvil.

10

Horse-Mother in a Mare-ternity Ward

When you are horse-mother in a mare-ternity ward you try to maintain an unblemished record for safe, hygienic deliveries.

In all of our foalings at the Bar None, Frank and I were happy to report, in every instance:

"Mother and child doing nicely!"

Then poor Dolly Dumpling broke our good record. Dolly was a Welsh pony that Frank bought from an itinerant dealer, for the best of all reasons: he felt sorry for her. Dolly was a sad-eyed, trusting little thing, ruggedly built, but with a heavenly disposition. She was meek and well broken but showed all the symptoms of misuse and neglect guaranteed to make her appear irresistible to my horse lover.

The dealer guaranteed her "open," that is, ready to breed and Frank planned to breed her to a pony-size Appaloosa Stud. (This was while we were still avid for spotted horses.) The off-spring of such matings, if loud colored and not more than fifty-two inches high, can be registered in the Pony of Americas Stud Book and command an exceptionally high price. When you see one you understand why. There is absolutely nothing more appealing than a pint-size horse, all of a color except for its rump, which looks as if it was splashed with white paint.

But just to prove that lightning can strike twice in the same place—or possibly to prove that you can't trust itinerant horse dealers—we discovered, when we had Dolly vet checked, that she was already in foal. Now history would repeat itself and we would go through what we went through with Big Mama. But surely we wouldn't find two girls mixed up about sex.

Dolly did not present us with the problem of a boy-girl filly or a girl-boy stud. She surprised us in different ways. For one thing, it turned out that she was well along in her pregnancy. She hadn't showed it because she was half-starved.

But as Frank poured grain into her she began to fill out, her bag became distended and we realized her foaling date was imminent.

One morning Frank looked in her stall and found her in labor.

Immediately he clanged the gong we use for an alarm signal.

I was stuffing a chicken at the time but I promptly shoved it in the refrigerator, yanked on my work boots and headed for the stables.

Dolly's water bag had broken and I saw a tiny pointed hoof emerging as I dropped at Frank's side, ready to act as mid-wife.

Dolly strained and strained but made no further progress.

Soon we realized what was causing her trouble. The second hoof had failed to appear. Examination showed that it was doubled back on itself in such a way that labor could not proceed until the foal's position was shifted so that the leg could be moved. With infinite patience and gentleness Frank worked to release the second hoof. The two front forelegs then emerged with the colt's head between them.

Since it was not a breech birth labor should have continued without further difficulty. But the shoulders of a foal are the largest part of its body, and we realized that Dolly was in the process of producing a foal much, much too large for her pony physique.

The reason was obvious. She must have been bred to a huge horse instead of to a pony her own size.

I called the vet immediately and went back to help Frank and we became so engrossed in our work that two hours passed before we realized that the vet was long overdue. We called him again and were told by his office that his car had broken down and his assistant was on his way to the Bar None. Meanwhile we would have to do what we could on our own.

Frank and I have delivered so many colts in tandem since we became horse breeders that we no longer panic no matter what develops. But we were far from experienced when Dolly ran into trouble and we were thoroughly frightened. Both of us could see that it would be impossible for Dolly's pony frame to accommodate the delivery of this gigantic foal.

A full hour later, when we finally managed to free the foal, little Dolly was so weak and exhausted that she lay stretched out, with her eyes closed, completely unaware of her youngster. We did everything we could to revive her, but within a few minutes she gave a great sigh and quietly expired.

The colt was weaving about on spindly legs but he too had suffered such an ordeal that he could remain standing for only a few seconds at a time; then down he'd thud.

He was a stud colt; jet black, with soulful dark eyes. But there his resemblance to any normal colt ended. He had the head of a moose, the legs of a kangaroo and his back was as wide as a whisker. He looked less like a horse than a mackerel.

"Oh you poor little monster, without a mother!" I said to myself and felt the tears slide down my face.

I brushed them aside with the back of my hand and glanced at Frank. His eyes were red and he was blowing his nose. I knew he felt every bit as badly as I did. I sniffed mightily and blinked and blinked but the tears wouldn't stop.

Just then the assistant vet arrived and took over.

He made arrangements to have Dolly removed from the ranch; he gave the poor staggering orphan a pick-up shot and told us to see if one of our other mares would allow the poor little motherless fellow to nurse.

The vet's entire schedule had been disrupted and he had to race off to another emergency and once again we were on our own.

We looked at our little orphan and wondered how he could possibly survive.

His hind legs were so weak that he couldn't walk on his hoofs. Instead he walked on his pasterns, with his feet turned straight up in the air.

"He can't be real," said Joan Benson when she arrived that morning to inspect the new arrival.

A catch in her voice made me look at her sharply and I saw that her face was as wet as my own.

"What will you name him?"

Naming a new colt was always such a joyous occasion I knew she was trying to cheer me. But there was no joy at the Bar None that morning.

"Sad Sam."

"Suits him perfectly," said Joan. "He has an expression that ties knots in your heart. But you shouldn't let his present condition determine his future character. He may turn out to be Glad Sam, for all you know."

"You're absolutely right!" I cried, feeling a return of my customary optimism. "We won't call him anything yet till we have time to get to know him."

"If he lives he'll be grateful to you," said Joan.

Her comment shocked me.

"What do you mean—IF he lives! Of course he'll live!"

"Have you tried getting any milk down him?"

"Not yet."

"Just how do you plan to do it?"

"Paleface is giving much more milk than her filly, Papoose, could possibly need. We'll see if she'll let Sam nurse her."

"Paleface is not exactly your friendliest mare," remarked Joan, puffing her cigarette thoughtfully.

This was certainly an understatement, since Paleface was over-protective toward her filly and lashed out with both heels at anyone who came near her.

"How about Big Mama?"

"You're right. We'll try her. She always gives enough milk for three."

"Let's see how we make out. Here comes Frank with Big Mama now."

Big Mama surprised us all by being thoroughly cantankerous. She refused to allow Sam within a foot of her milk supply and caught him in the flank with a pie plate hoof that sent him flying.

"Well, what do we do now?" I asked Frank after we struggled for over an hour, until Sam finally lay down and refused to get up again.

"Let's get some calf nurser and one of those half-gallon calf nursing bottles and see how that works," said Frank.

"Good idea. I'm going in town and I'll bring them back for you," offered Joan, and she swung into her little pink jeep with the fringe on top and screeched off in a cloud of dust.

When she returned we followed directions carefully and mixed a nursing bottle of calf nurser and water for Sam.

We thought we would have trouble getting him to take the bottle but he attacked it with such gusto that the contents were drained in no time.

"If he nurses like this we won't have any problem," I exulted.

But I hadn't figured on one thing. Sam was a colt, not a calf. Cow's milk has much more butter fat content and much less sugar content than mare's milk and our calf formula did not sit well at all with Sam. Though he took his bottle readily, the contents played havoc with his digestive system.

Within twelve hours the dread signs of "scours" (the name for infant diarrhea among animals) appeared.

Sam was physicked to the point of dehydration and soon became too weak to stagger around. His little black butt became raw and red as an infant's bottom and we had to wash him down with tincture of green soap after each bowel movement, and this meant several bathings within each hour.

"He can't possibly live."

"Once they scour that bad they're done for."

"No colt in that shape could possibly make it, you'd better give up."

These were the comforting opinions expressed by those who beheld Sam.

And he was a sight to behold. He had lost weight until his body resembled a skeleton. Every rib showed and his flanks were so hollow they met in the middle.

My heart sank every time I looked at him but I would not give up. I kept thinking of his mother and the way she had lifted her head just before she died for one fleeting glimpse of him and I knew I had to keep Sam alive because we owed Dolly that much.

But we could never have saved Sam if it hadn't been for a dear friend of ours who delivered our laundry to the ranch.

Lola Gart was a comfortable farm woman from Iowa and she had once raised a work colt on the bottle.

"It isn't easy," she said, "And your critter looks beyond saving. But there's a trick to it. Throw that cow's milk formula away and do as I tell you."

We followed her instructions exactly and mixed one can of evaporated milk with an equal quantity of warm water. We added three tablespoonsful of sugar, a quarter of a cup of kaopectate and a dash of salt. Since Sam drank any liquid offered to him, it was easy to switch him to his new formula.

And, still following Lola's orders, we gave him a bottle every four hours, right around the clock.

It had been a long time since we'd gotten up for a two o'clock feeding and it was a two-legged young-un and not a four-legged one that had demanded our attention in that dim, distant past. But our hand had never lost its skill.

When we reached his stall in the middle of the night, Sam would be snuffling and whinnying, eager for his bottle, for the scours had left him half-starved.

Within twenty-four hours the diarrhea stopped. He began to pick up. And, still obeying Lola, we added a raw egg to each of Sam's bottles. He was now getting six bottles and six eggs a day.

His eyes brightened; his coat glistened. He became so strong that I had to brace myself with both feet and hang onto the bottle for dear life when I extended it to him because he could pull on it with the force of a Mack truck and he could empty it so fast that he threatened to turn it inside out if you didn't get it way from him before the last mouthful.

Once night feedings had been abandoned, it became my task to handle the day feedings solo. By now Sam began to associate me with milk and motherhood to such a degree that he never saw me without whinnying and whinkering; and he would try to climb the fence in order to get to me.

I had only to open the kitchen door and he would paw at the corral rail, curl his nose, and sniff for his milk. And he would kick the fence down if it didn't materialize fast enough to suit him.

To say that a bond had been established between us would be stating it mildly. Sam had a mother complex and I was the object of it.

If I went near Sam without a bottle he tried to suck my fingers, my hat, my jacket, or my boot tops—whichever happened to be handiest.

I looked at my bony beastie, with his kangaroo legs and his

moose head and his rapidly developing carcass, and I wondered if, in attempting to fulfill my obligation to Dolly, I had over-played the role of foster mother.

Sam had acquired a new name as he became robust and raucous.

His latest appellation was "Sam, the Monster."

And he loved me with a frightening devotion.

Shades of Oedipus!

I knew that somehow I had to wean Sam and get him started on dry feed or I'd have him tied to my jeans forever. I received no sympathy from anyone else on the ranch.

"You made him a monster with your doting care, now cope with him," was their kindly advice.

And so I spent hours with Sam trying to coax a little dry feed down his gullet. He would lie outstretched in the sun and I would sit with his head in my lap, patiently trying to force a few grains of feed at a time between his flabby lips.

Most of it he would spit back out, so that progress was ex-tremely slow—possibly one grain of feed out of a hundred would reach its destination.

Sometimes Sam would let the feed enter his mouth and he'd roll it around on his tongue and I'd think he was chewing it. Five minutes later it would roll out the other side of his mouth untouched.

After countless days of this cajolery he finally began to take sufficient interest in his feed to chew it. Then he began to like it. Next he looked forward to it and eventually he demanded it.

When he was taking a pound of dry feed each day I began cutting back on his bottles and in two weeks he was off his formula.

Sam turned out to be the most un-handsome horse we ever owned.

Anyone seeing him for the first time invariably bursts out laughing and then cries: "What is that! A horse or a kangaroo?"

Sometimes they vary the question and want to know if Sam is a horse or a moose.

"He is our Sam," we reply with dignity, "and we love him. He may be an Ugly Duckling but he has a noble character."

This is an out-and-out lie because Sam is ornery as they come.

His trouble is that he imagines he is people since he was raised by people and treated like people and has never known any other parents but people.

Therefore he is highly indignant if he isn't treated like people.

He shuns the other horses but will follow Frank or me any place. And when he follows he does not remain at a respectful distance but climbs on top of us. And since he has known only love and is thoroughly spoiled, Sam is not afraid of anything nor have we ever been able to make him afraid of anything, even a whip.

If you strike him with one, as you must occasionally in order to keep him from sitting on top of you, he gives you a puzzled look and ignores the chastisement.

If you go out in the field with him he immediately attaches himself to you, breathing down your back, or looking soulfully into your eyes; and no amount of cussing or rock-throwing or whip-lashing or abject entreaty has any effect on him; he simply remains attached to you.

By the time he was two, Sam was already twice the size of his mother so we know his father must have been Mighty Horse. But it is impossible to train him to do anything because of his imperviousness to any punishment and it is just as impossible to sell him because no one sees his hidden beauty as we do.

And so we believed that Dolly's son, Sam, would be with us forever.

One day our hopes were raised when a man came to the ranch, looked at Sam and put a deposit on him, intending to buy him.

The man never came back.

We decided we'd always have Sam because nobody else would ever appreciate him. But there we were wrong.

A man did eventually buy Sam for his son and told us later that Sam made an excellent kid's horse after he broke him.

Since I've always felt a special affinity for our little black Sambo I coaxed Frank into taking me to see him one day since he'd only moved to a neighboring ranch.

The little boy was riding Sam in a field when we drove up in the Camino and as soon as we stepped out of the car Sam saw us; or scented me, I'm not sure which.

He promptly dropped his shoulder in a tricky movement that neatly dumped the little boy off and came flying toward me, whinnying, with his tail up and his nose curled, the way he used to do when I came toward him with his feeding bottle.

I jumped in the Camino just in time to escape his huge slobbery kiss, but he wouldn't leave me. He kept trying to get his huge head in through the window and would paw at the door and finally we had to drive away.

The boy's father had to forcibly restrain Sam to keep him from tagging after me.

I waved to the big oaf through a diamond splash of tears.

"I really should go on television," I told Frank, as we pulled away from the neighbor's ranch. "I've got a secret: I'm the mother of a horse."

11

Lady, Endomorph With a Beautiful Soul

Lady is queen of the ranch.

She is the only dog at the Bar None.

We have had opportunities to acquire more shapely dogs and certainly more highly bred dogs, but we prefer Lady.

Lady is more than a friend. She is a venerated member of the family.

Lady's ancestry is a subject she does not like us to touch upon and we respect her feeling in this matter.

The man from the county who issues dog licenses has declared, on record, that she is a cross between a Beagle and a Golden Retriever. We are happy to let it go at that.

If he is right, it would account for Lady's delicately cast, finely boned head and her pendulous, over-sized body.

It would also explain her warm, golden color and her brown, spice drop of a nose.

There are emotional reasons for Lady's vast avoirdupois.

Lady is an endomorph. The vet says this means she is viscera-oriented. In people talk, she has a penchant for food.

Lady licks plates clean, does away with table scraps and scoops crumbs off the floor with the dexterity and purposefulness of a vacuum cleaner.

120

Lady does this because she is obsessed by an insatiable hunger. It is a hunger for children which Lady, alas, cannot have.

Lady's former owners had her spayed while she was still a puppy. We have no idea why and we have no idea who the wretches were.

Frank and our son, B.G., returned from town one day with Lady seated proudly between them on the front seat of the Camino.

They had found her at our local service station.

She was sleeping in a telephone booth and living on crank case oil.

Her former owners had dropped her off out of a car, sped away and never returned for her. Lady was such a tiny little thing the day Frank and B.G. presented her to me, I had no idea what she would become.

The diet of crank case oil should have given us a clue. Lady has been part of the family for over a decade, and in that time she has eaten enough chicken bones, lamb bones, ham bones, and debris to fill a pick-up. She has also dined on chicken feed, horse feed, cat feed, and calf feed—in addition to her regular rations of dog feed.

Since we are not completely insensitive to the welfare of our animal companions, we have tried, over the years, to put Lady on a reducing diet.

We've talked with our vet and given her everything he recommended from concentrated protein to starvation diets.

As soon as our backs are turned Lady steals food from all the other ranch residents including the ground squirrels. She digs up their secret caches. And, when all else fails, she is not above consuming horse manure, which, the vet assures us, is an excellent source of pre-digested nutriment.

When we capitulate, as we invariably do, and say: "To heck with diets. Lady has only one pleasure in life, which is eating, so we may as well let her indulge it," Lady enjoys life again.

She eats everything we give her. Then she makes a tour of the ranch, and snitches something from each of the animals in turn. Then she snitches milk from the cats. And when she has gorged herself till she reaches a stage of happy stupefaction she digs up all the old mouldy bones she has previously buried against the day of deprivation, and gnaws at them till she reduces them to powder.

Between courses Lady sluices down gallons of water and complains bitterly if copious amounts aren't readily available.

Those who behold Lady for the first time frequently exclaim: "What is that, a dog or a pig?"

Then they burst into rude, raucous laughter.

These people are not the sort I choose for friends.

Lady may be broad as she is long; she may resemble a knackwurst with toothpicks for legs; but Lady has a beautiful soul.

You can see the beauty of Lady's soul when you look in her liquid brown eyes. They glow with love and reflect Lady's keen interest in the human race. Lady observes the antics of those around her with a tender, compassionate tolerance.

In all the years that she has lived with us Lady has never expressed anything but love to us and to everyone associated with us.

Lady never growls or snaps at anyone; though many of the people who laugh at her so raucously are given to growling and snapping.

Before our son joined the Navy, while he was still a teenager, life at the Bar None was not always a tranquil experience. Many times the entire household would be in an uproar as we went through the various stages of cycling, surfing, clandestine smoking, and drag racing.

Tempers would flare, voices would rise and angry blows would fall on blue-jeaned bottoms.

At such times, when I would pop my cork and find myself making the banshee-like sounds of an angry mother—very unlovely sounds, actually—I would feel Lady's presence and look up to behold her gentle brown eyes fixed on me questioningly.

I knew only too well what she was thinking.

"Is this clamor necessary? Isn't there a loving way to handle the situation? Now, if I had children . . ."

My face would flush before that thoughtful gaze; my voice descend; equanimity would soon be restored.

If Lady had been blessed with children she would be a perfect mother, administering a firm but loving discipline with patience and understanding.

Frank does not scatter his affection among the ranch animals as I do.

He tolerates the cats, educates the horses, castigates the chickens (when they deposit chicken doo on his tobacco pouch), and manages to ignore flowers, cloud formations, and birds.

But Frank loves Lady.

Frank finds Lady's companionship superior to that of many women because, as he says, when she barks she usually has something important to say.

This is true. Lady is not given to idle yapping. But night or day, if a horse misbehaves or a colt slips out of a corral, or water is left running or a gate unlocked, Lady gives tongue, since she considers it her duty to call misdemeanors to our attention.

When Lady still had a figure and was fairly young and agile, she always accompanied Frank and me whenever we went horseback riding over the ranch. She kept ahead of the horses, her curling, golden tail frantic with excitement, sniffing at gopher holes and scaring rabbits out of the brush.

On one such sortie she managed to catch her paw in a spring trap which a neighboring rancher had set out for foxes. That was one of the many times I was both proud and thankful that I married a Horse Lover. One who knows his way around outdoors and doesn't panic in an emergency.

Frank held on to his horse's reins—this in spite of the fact that the horse was frantic with fear at the sight of Lady's flopping and flailings. And while the horse snorted and chomped and Lady thrashed about and howled, Frank managed to grab Lady by the scruff of her neck, pin her down, and release the pressure of the trap with his foot.

Mercifully Lady's leg was not broken; but she seldom went with us on our riding excursions after her traumatic experience. And now, of course, she can barely circumnavigate the back yard.

Lady is not fond of cats. She begrudges them every scrap of food they eat. She knows better than to steal their feed in my presence but she will sit, brown nose on her paws, and watch them eat, her brow wrinkled queruously.

But even though she has an aversion to cats, Lady has a soft spot in her heart for Slinky, my pet cat, because Slinky saved her life.

One day a vicious police dog found his way to the ranch. Usually Lady ignores strange dogs, not having any amorous interest in them. But for some reason she growled at this particular dog and instantly he laced into her, pinned her to the ground and seized her by the throat.

Lady lay on her back, legs to the sky, a hunk of helpless blubber, unable to right herself. In a few seconds the dog would have finished her off. But just then Slinky, who is really a mush and not at all aggressive toward dogs, hurled himself at the dog, and sank his claws in its back.

The dog fled, howling.

Since then Lady regards Slinky, if not with affection, at least with respect. But it irks her to see Slinky curl up in my lap.

Like most fat girls, Lady imagines she's slimmer than she is. She is convinced that she'd make a good lap dog.

Lady may not be able to do the Frug, the Jackrabbit or the Jerk but she's a whizz at the Itch and does it constantly during Flea Season.

Built as she is, with folds and furrows of fat across the

rump, Lady provides a perfect hideout for fleas. Lady's fleas multiply in an endless geometric progression and live high on the hog, so to speak—though I'm sure Lady would not approve of that expression—and the reason they have such a ball is because Lady is so fat she just can't get at the fleas to dislodge them.

She can't reach her rump to bite it so she bites her paws. She chewed all the flesh off one paw before I figured out what was wrong. Then it finally dawned on me that Lady was trying to kill her fleas by proxy—and of course it didn't work.

As soon as we discovered what was bothering Lady we clipped her right down to her hide with the horse clippers. She looked like a little blonde lioness but she was so embarrassed by her nudity if anyone laughed at her she would run off and hide under the hay.

But we found that clipping gave Lady only temporary relief from her fleas. They soon returned. And that's when I really went to work. I hosed Lady down, lathered her with Flea Soap, rinsed her in a solution of Sheep Dip, dried her thoroughly, and powdered her generously with flea powder. Then I disinfected her sleeping quarters.

By following this rugged ritual I managed to keep the fleas off Lady at least for a week. Then I had to start over again.

Lady would have to be dragged to her de-fleaing station, sad-eyed and protesting, but she would emerge from the ordeal playful and prankish as a baby hippo.

Frank says that Lady is his dog.

Till it is time to deflea her.

Then I slip and slop, splash and gurgle, stand on my head, with perspiration running into my eyes and off the end of my nose and swear I'll never go through the agony again—Lady can just learn to live with her fleas—then Lady gives me the doe-eyed, woe-is-me look and I battle the fleas again. One wave of delight from her little curling tail at the end of our seance and I know the whole shmear is worth it.

As Lady grows older she becomes more and more insistent on having her creature comforts. During a heat wave, when we turn on the air conditioner, she immediately thwops at the back door demanding to be admitted. She then sprawls in a blob on the kitchen floor, in the path of the frosty breezes.

On the other hand, at the first hint of cold she pulls her blanket over to the wood stove where she can thaw her old bones in comfort.

Lady has taken to snoring in her sunset years. Not ordinary snores, but cataclysmic sonic buffetings that vibrate throughout the entire house. Once Frank tiptoed through the house with his shot gun cocked, imagining the little people from Mars had descended; but the noise he heard was Lady snoring.

Lady is the only dog our son, B.G., has ever known.

She was his companion through all his growing-up years and I can see her now, racing beside his bike; trotting after his ball, tramping beside him over the ranch hills; B.G. toting his air rifle, Lady snuffling and snorting at his side.

I've never been in sympathy with hunting. But I never had to worry about B.G. shooting anything as long as Lady was with him. She made enough noise to warn the game away for miles around.

As B.G. grew older and cycles and surf boards, cars and gals became more intriguing to him than hiking and hunting with Lady, it would have been easy to imagine that he had lost some of his affection for his childhood pet.

But when we said goodbye to B.G. the day he enlisted in the Navy, the last thing he said as he walked away from us toward the recruiting building was:

"Keep Lady alive at least three more years, till I finish my first hitch, will you, Mom?"

"I'll try," I promised, through a mist of tears.

And thus far I've managed to do it!

12

Bubbles,

The Girl Who Had Troubles

There are times at the Bar None when the help is so restless and the turnover so rapid that, in retrospect, it is difficult to recall either the names or the faces of those who for long stretches live closer than kin to us.

Such a period followed the departure of the fair Felice. Women, single or with husbands, were not to work on the ranch, Frank declared. And so the next hand to take over the care of the horses was Glamis McCurdle, a dour, lantern-jawed gentleman from the Aulde Sod.

Frank suspected Glamis of being cruel to the horses because they all became head shy right after he joined us. Also, it was no secret that Glamis sipped the sauce. He sipped it, he said, to drown his wicked conscience, which had not stopped tormenting him since his wife died.

Glamis's drinking had driven his wife to an early grave, and raw, corrosive guilt built a fire under Glamis every day, which only the sauce could extinguish.

Glamis slept in his cabin (Frank told me) *au naturelle;*

127

leaving the fireplace blazing, the oil stove blasting, and all the windows wide open.

To make sure that the fire would be raging hot, Glamis sneaked logs cut from telephone poles into the cabin. We used such logs for fence replacements but never for firewood because they were coated with creosote which flares like kerosene the instant a match touches it. Frank forbade Glamis to use the telephone poles in the fireplace but he continued to smuggle them in whenever Frank's back was turned.

One night, Frank made a routine "lights out" inspection and heard a roar coming from Glamis's retreat. He burst in to find Glamis passed out on the floor and flames springing from the fireplace high as the ceiling.

Glamis had tossed one of the creosoted logs in the fire and then folded up.

Belchings from the fireplace filled the cabin with smoke and it was only by sheer luck that Frank managed to seize the burning log (he was wearing heavy work gloves at the time) and toss it out the window where it fell on a pile of sand left there for masonry repair work.

I came running with the ever-ready fire extinguisher in response to Frank's howls and together we soon had things under control.

Glamis slept peacefully through the whole incident.

Next day Frank sent him packing.

My memories of Glamis are less than cordial since it took me a week to repaint the smoke-stained cabin after his departure.

Glamis was followed by a tall, sere, dolorous individual named Earnest. And earnest he was. He was also remarkably honest. When asked if he imbibed Earnest replied: "Yes, sir. I do. But never to excess. Drinking has never interfered with my work and it never will. If you find that it does you may fire me."

Frank was touched by such refreshing forthrightness.

He hired Earnest. And all the while that Earnest worked for us we never saw him drunk. In fairness, I must add that we never saw him sober. Earnest drank privately, expertly, quietly, and constantly. His eyes were sometimes glazed and his speech sometimes fuddled; but Earnest remained at his post.

We never knew what Earnest drank. We never knew when Earnest drank. We never knew where Earnest drank. But we did know that Earnest was always pleasantly potted.

Earnest was what is known among horsemen as an "easy keeper." He had no interest in food but lived on coffee, cigarettes, and the nectar of the gods. He had the oyster-blue complexion of the chronic tippler and was so emaciated that his clothes flapped about him. But even when thoroughly juiced Earnest remained always, Earnest. He performed his chores silently and with a certain dedicated thoroughness. And the more he drank the more meticulous he became in the execution of his duties.

If he went near the hayloft he carefully dinched his cigarette.

If he watered the stock he made two or three trips back to the faucet to make sure he'd shut the water off.

If he brought the colts in from pasture he would totteringly retrace his steps to see if he'd remembered to lock the gate.

If it hadn't been for the pungency of his breath and the shakiness of his gait it would have been impossible to believe that Earnest imbibed constantly. Especially since we never found any evidence of what he drank or where he drank it.

Then one day Frank had occasion to tear down some outbuildings, including an old privy that had become an eye-sore on the ranch. There, in the excavation beneath the two-seater, he found sixty-four one-gallon wine jugs. One for each day that Earnest had been with us. Where he got them, how he smuggled them onto the ranch and conveyed them to the privy, or where he consumed them, will ever remain a mystery.

But now we knew Earnest was a wino.

We were sorry indeed, for his sake. And for ours. Because in spite of his devotion to the juice Earnest was one of the most dependable hands we ever had.

Toward spring, however, Earnest began to show signs of the wanderlust. We are all too familiar with the symptoms. And once they appear we know that we had best resign ourselves to the inevitable progression of events which follow.

First there is a petulant complaint about even the simplest chore where before there was an eager desire to tackle it.

The petulance increases until nothing appears satisfactory to a hand who formerly praised everyone and everything around him.

With Earnest the patter ran this way:

"Don't see how a body can sleep in a place where the danged birds chirp their fool heads off every morning!"

"Fella gets mighty sick of corn bread and spareribs, I can tell you!"

"Plenty lonesome stuck out here with nothin' but critters to tend to day after day!"

We'd heard these lyrics before. And, hearing them now, we realized that Earnest didn't have long for the ranch.

Sure enough, he gave his notice and told Frank to get someone to replace him. Then immediately his spirits rose. He talked with longing of visiting his cronies on Skid Row where you could get "The best goldang hot dogs this side of the Pecos."

Earnest left the Bar None one sweet spring morning when the mountain lilacs spread their lavender garlands across the fading green of the mountains, and the valleys were stained with blue ink spots of cloud shadows.

He looked at the mares, who were heavy in foal, and brushed away a tear from his pale, red-rimmed eye.

"Won't get to see the young-uns," he said, sadly. His Adam's apple slid up, then down, past the lump in his throat. Then he brightened, shook my hand with his dry, hard, calloused one, pulled his cap down hard over his nose, and stepped off jauntily down the road. He carried his possessions in a paper sack and listed slightly to the right.

We waved till he was only a dot in the lane. We were sorry to see Earnest leave. And so were the horses. They whinnied and thrust their heads over the fence rails as his thin form

Frank counted two hundred and seventeen wine bottles that Earnest left behind when he loaded them in the Camino for

trudged by.

I slipped one out to use as a candle holder for the patio.

burial.

Sometimes, when a candle sputters above it, I imagine I can see Earnest's thin form curled within it; sealed inside like a skeletal ship, never to escape.

"No couples at the ranch!"

Frank speaking.

The outburst was occasioned by my timid suggestion that perhaps it might be good to get in touch with the man at the state employment office now that the colts were due.

"We'll do the work ourselves," cried Frank. "I'll help you in the kitchen and you help me in the paddock."

I said no more about help for a while. The thought of Frank making corn pone was even more frightening than the prospect of me shoveling horse "doo-doos." Frank knows absolutely nothing about cooking and I know absolutely nothing about a horse. Only what I've absorbed by psychological osmosis as the result of listening to horsemen.

Still, at the Bar None there are always chores and more chores and so . . .

Buster and Bubbles Glutz set up housekeeping with us as a ranch couple.

Buster Glutz was soft-eyed, soft-spoken; a docile fellow, with a gentle, submissive disposition.

When Frank interviewed him he didn't mention that he was married.

After Frank agreed to hire him the state employment man

called and said a wife went with him. He described the couple as honest and reliable and desperately in need of work. He said he could recommend them without reservation as animal lovers and steady hands.

Bubbles and Buster appeared at the Bar None in a ramshackle car which just made it to the door of their cabin. There it died. This seemed not to upset Buster in the least. He said he'd fix it on his first day off.

Bubbles emerged from the car in shabby ranch pants and a nondescript man's shirt. She had her hair in rollers which were swathed in a grimy handkerchief. She was a tiny but curvaceous little woman of indeterminate age, with myopic eyes, a petulant expression, and a not unfriendly manner.

She was followed by a robust young German Shepherd pup with a rich black coat, a finely plumed tail and a not unfriendly manner.

The dog was on a leash and Bubbles hugged him close to her side.

"What a beautiful dog," I cried, extending a hand to him. He licked it with a big, lolling tongue, whimpered and thumped his tail on the ground. I loved him instantly.

Frank caught sight of the dog and came over for a closer inspection.

"What unusual ears your dog has," I said to Bubbles, after introductions. Frank's eyebrows were flashing storm signals so I tried to keep the conversation going. "I don't think I've ever seen a German Shepherd with ears quite like his."

"He isn't a German Shepherd," said Bubbles. She had a sharp, purse-lipped way of speaking. "His mother was a full-blooded coyote and his father was a Malamute."

Involuntarily I withdrew my hand from the slobbering jaws. But the friendship in those honest brown eyes was sincere. I patted him again. At that instant we esablished a relationship of mutual trust.

"We can't have a dog like that around young stock," said

Frank. He said it in his "no nonsense" voice. "I should have been told about this dog before you came here."

"Bubbles wouldn't let me tell you. She said if you knew about the dog you wouldn't hire us," said Buster with a big grin. "Ask her what his name is. Go ahead."

"What's his name?" I asked obligingly.

"Troubles."

"Ask her why," guffawed Buster.

"Why don't you let us guess?"

"I call him Troubles because he's lost us every job we ever got," said Bubbles with candor.

"Well I think he's lost you this one before you got it," said Frank. "We have a lot of young colts due and I can't trust a dog like that around them. You'd better get that car fixed and get out of here as fast as you can."

"Why did Troubles lose you your job?" I asked Bubbles.

"Because people wanted us to keep him tied all the time and I won't. So we left."

"Is that the only reason?"

"That's right," said Buster. "Troubles never did nothin' mean in his life. He loves people and animals and ain't never chased any stock or hurt nothin' yet. He wouldn't even hurt a chicken or a baby kitten."

"If you don't believe it, watch," said Bubbles, and before we could stop her she unleashed the dog.

He loped off, making a circle of the ranch yard, sniffing at the trail of the chickens, the guineas, the cats and the colts, then returned to Bubbles and plopped down beside her. The cats did not head for the trees as they frequently do when strange dogs come to the ranch and the chickens continued their clucking and pecking, as did the guineas, undisturbed by Troubles' presence.

"He just likes to get out and run some. I can't bear to keep him cooped up all the time," said Bubbles and there were genuine tears in her eyes.

I was completely sold on Troubles myself and didn't believe he had it in him to harm anyone. But as I glanced toward Frank I saw his face was a thundercloud.

"I'll be responsible for Troubles and I won't let him do anything to cause any trouble," said Bubbles. "Just give him a chance. Don't make me take him back in town, he hates town life. Please let us stay. He'll be good. I promise. He needs to be outdoors . . ."

"And we need this job something dreadful," said Buster.

"Give them a chance, Frank," I pleaded. "We'll know in a day or two if the dog is all right."

"Sure, after it's too late and he's crippled one of the colts," said Frank.

Frank was right, I knew, and I was wrong. But Troubles was such a beautiful dog. I knew he couldn't be bad. I staked my reputation on it.

"You can stay till you get the car fixed or till the dog does something he shouldn't do," snapped Frank and stomped off. His pipe was sending up warning signals.

"Thanks," said Bubbles.

"Thanks," said Buster.

Troubles licked my hand.

I'd really done it this time.

What if Troubles ruined one of Frank's valuable colts? Why should I suddenly develop this ridiculous attachment to Troubles, son of White Fang?

"Better not unpack too many things," I cautioned the Glutzes as they dragged their battered lares and penates out of the beat-up car.

"And you'd better have that car ready to roll in case Frank flips his lid."

Impulsively Bubbles flung her arms around me and planted a sloppy kiss on my cheek. "You'll never be sorry you trusted Troubles," she said dramatically. "Troubles will be your friend forever!"

At this point Frank came stomping back.

"Let's get one thing straight right now, Glutz," he said to Buster. "That dog is to be tied whenever we're exercising the colts or currying them and whenever anyone is mounting or dismounting from a horse or when strangers with children come to look at the horses."

"Oh you bet. Yes sir," cried Buster.

"I don't want him tied when . . ." began Bubbles but Buster let her have a left heel to the shin.

As I followed Frank's angry back to the house I heard Buster mutter to Bubbles: "Keep the dog tied when he says to and we may be able to keep this job, idiot!"

"I'm not going to keep Troubles tied up, that's why I brought him out of the city," she retorted.

Buster was carrying a pillow toward the cabin and he flung it at Bubbles, cutting off the rest of the sentence.

Bubbles also smuggled in, with her belongings, a Parakeet named Jasper, a baby Siamese kitten named Charlie Chan, and a huge aquarium filled with water and STONES.

When I asked her why she had no fish in it she said the cat always ate them and she preferred an aquarium without fish as it was easier to move. She could just dump the water out, load it up and refill it when they reached the next job.

"It hasn't been easy," she confided, "losing six jobs in six months on account of Troubles. Buster gets pretty het up. But I told him if he wants me Troubles goes with me and he can't have one without the other, job or no job."

A girl who loves animals this way can't be all bad, I thought; there's tenderness somewhere beneath that gruff exterior. But why couldn't she express a little of it toward Buster, her husband?

For Buster, Bubbles had only brusque insults, hard glances, and strident criticism. But he took it all smiling.

"Bubbles is a very nervous woman," he told me one day

when I met him standing outside the cabin door trying to summon up sufficient courage to go in. "Ever since she lost the baby she hasn't been the same."

"Oh did poor Bubbles lose a baby recently?" I asked, understanding only too well how such an experience might have left its mark.

"Not exactly recently," said Buster, bending to remove a wad of manure from the heel of his cowboy boot. He pried it loose with one finger, then wiped the finger on the heel of his other boot. "We lost the baby thirteen years ago but she just never got over it. That's why I was happy to get her Troubles. It sort of took her mind off it. She loves that dog," he said wistfully, as if wishing just a little of Bubbles' love might be left over for him.

"She isn't keeping Troubles tied the way she promised and I just hope Mr. Griffith will let you both stay," I said gently.

After the first day Bubbles had allowed Troubles to run loose all over the ranch. Then she spent most of her time yelling to him in a voice that could be heard past the north forty: "Troubles! Troubles." The word had become a sort of *leitmotif* for all the other sounds at the ranch.

Buster's face turned red.

"I honest can't get her to tie him. But he really won't hurt nothin'," he said sorrowfully.

"I know it. And Troubles knows it. But we have to convince Mr. Griffith, Buster. If I were you I'd tell Bubbles to tie him at least when someone's working around the green colts."

"Yes'm," sighed Buster and took a deep breath and went inside the cabin.

I had never seen Bubbles dressed in anything but her faded jeans and her sloppy sweat shirt with her hair in rollers and bound in a scarf.

Therefore I was astonished to see her emerge from the cabin

on Sunday dressed in tan English riding pants, stretched tighter than her hide; a fitted suit jacket with a fur collar; and pink sequined cowboy boots. Her hair, which she had finally unbound, flamed in an excited red cloud to her waist and in it she had twined butterflies, ropes of pearls and tiny velvet bows.

"Why, Bubbles," I gasped, trying to make my exclamation sound admiring, "You *are* dressed up! Where are you going?"

"To visit Buster's folks. Buster's got the car running with the parts Mr. Griffith brought him from town so we can make it easily. They only live a hundred and fifty miles from here."

The thought of driving their poor asthmatic car three hundred miles in one day sounded like sheerest cruelty but I withheld comment.

"Are you taking Troubles with you?" I asked hopefully, wondering what I'd do if they should leave him and the car gave up the ghost.

"No. I'm leaving him in the cabin. He'll lie there quiet till we get back. I left feed and water near him. You might take a look inside later but don't let him out because if anything ever happened to that dog I'd kill myself and Buster knows it."

I could understand how a woman who had grieved thirteen years for a lost baby might easily develop an over-attachment for a dog, so once more I withheld comment.

"I won't let anything happen to Troubles," I said. "I love him. And I'm inclined to think he has a warm spot in his heart for me."

"Come on if you're coming," called Buster from the car.

"Shut up, you hair-brained idiot," bellowed Bubbles in her dog-calling voice. "You won't know enough if you live to be a hundred to boss me around."

Poor Buster. He took every bellow with high good humor, knowing that the flares and the flashes from Bubbles were simply sound and fury hiding the ache of a mother's heart broken in brittle pieces.

The Glutzes hadn't been gone an hour when I began worrying about Troubles. I hated to think of him cooped up inside the cabin because I knew he loved to be outdoors. Every day he followed Bubbles as she followed Buster at his chores. Finally I could stand it no longer. Without saying anything to Frank I slipped in the cabin to see how Troubles was making out.

He was curled in a ball on top of Bubbles' bed, surrounded by a variety of toys that Bubbles had made for him. Stuffed frogs, puppies, kittens, even fish lay all around him. When he saw me he leaped off the bed and came toward me, wagging his entire rear end and whimpering a greeting.

I sat down on the floor beside him, patted him, and offered him one of the grubby toys to play with. As he chewed on it I glanced around the cabin.

It has never ceased to amaze me the way each new inhabitant manages to re-make the cabin so that it becomes a reflection of his personailty.

When Glamis lived in the cabin it was a pig sty. In fact it took several bottles of Clorox to remove the Glamis stench.

Earnest left the cabin austere and aseptic as a cloister.

And now Bubbles had given it all the flamboyancy of a brothel.

The aquarium, with its load of dank stones, stood on a window sill, the water within it muddy and turgid.

The parakeet did nip-ups and roll-overs in his cage, which was almost completely encased in a violent red coverall embroidered with pink seguins.

At the windows, Bubbles had hung shocking pink curtains made from dyed bath towels. These, too, were embroidered with sequins.

Near the bed lay a shag rug, obviously hand-loomed. It flamed a brilliant scarlet.

On top of the bed sprawled a chrocheted afghan in a violent paisley combination, predominantly purple.

Since I happen to be a color-sensitive individual who twangs to the slightest color clash, one who feels safe only with the quietest earth tones, I was ready to flee from the cabin. But I stared fascinated, at the lavishness of Bubbles' handiwork. Embroidery, appliqué, crocheting, knitting—there didn't seem to be anything in the needlework department that this brash little spitfire couldn't do.

Could it be that this was a way of assuaging the persistent, unconquerable pain of the lost baby? If so I resolved then and there to encourage Bubbles' craft work and to get her some things to work on next time I went in town.

As I started to leave, Troubles sat up on his haunches, pawed the air, and made heartrending noises deep in his throat.

The Glutzes would be gone several hours. Would he stay with me if I let him out?

If anything happened to him—I shuddered. Bubbles was just temperamental and histrionic enough to carry out any threat that might torture Buster.

But Troubles was so sweet and we seemed to have such an affinity for each other. I'd take a chance.

I let him out.

I spent the rest of the day trying to placate Frank and keep Troubles in sight. No matter what I did I knew I had to keep my mind on him. If he slipped out of my sight for a moment I would bellow, as loudly and raucously as Bubbles: "Troubles! Troubles!"

My constant bellowing irked Frank so much that he got on a horse and rode off to check fencing, leaving me to bellow by myself.

Usually after several minutes of bellowing I would find Troubles lying quietly under a bush watching me.

"Put that dog back in their cabin!" Frank commanded, at dusk, when I went to get dinner. "You know if anything happens to him that girl will be like a wild thing!"

How well I knew it. But Troubles was so sweet and I really enjoyed him so much. I hated to put him back in the cabin by himself.

"I'll bring him in the house with us," I compromised, "And I'll put him back in the cabin after dinner."

After dinner I decided to let him have one more romp while I checked to see if all the colts had water.

He loped around me, running off and coming back to me in a series of bounding parabolas.

"No wonder Bubbles loves him," I thought. "What a pity that they shouldn't be able to find a job just because some people have a thing about coyotes!"

One of the colts hooked a hoof in the corral wire and by the time I freed him and mended the wire I had forgotten Troubles completely.

As I reached the back door I realized with a shock, it must be at least twenty minutes since I had seen him or heard him and now it was pitch dark.

My heart dropped to the pit of my stomach.

"Troubles!" I bawled.

No response whatsoever.

"Troubles!" I bellowed like a cow when her calf gets away from her.

"Troubles!"

I sounded like Bubbles, doubled and tripled. And though I howled till my lungs ached and my voice cracked on the edge of hoarseness, I didn't want Frank to hear me. Fortunately he was inside watching the news on television and this gave me a respite.

I got a flashlight out of the ranch truck and began climbing the hills, crawling through the bushes.

"Troubles!"

"Troubles!"

Still no answer.

The search was hopeless and I knew it. There were a million

and one places he could have run to; an endless number of caves and woodpiles and feed stacks where he could be hiding.

My legs were trembling with weariness; my side had a stitch in it. I was perspiring, though the desert air had turned sharp with frost when the sun set. And now I had to face Frank . . . and later Bubbles . . . without Troubles.

I could only hope that wherever he was he would tire of this game of hide and seek and come back. I'd wait a half hour and then I'd call him again.

As I staggered into the house Frank met me.

"Where the devil have you been? I just missed you and was coming to . . . "

"Blackjack had a hoof in the fence. I got him out and fixed it."

"Why didn't you call me?"

(Thank goodness the television had drowned out my bleatings for Troubles!)

"I managed all right."

"You sure look beat. Come have a cup of coffee."

Temperamental, unpredictable Bubbles. What would she do? She'd want to hurt someone. Would she hurt Buster? Herself? I didn't care what she did to me. Whatever she did, I deserved it.

Just then I heard the gasping, wheezing sound of the Alutzes' car in the drive.

"Frank!"

Frank recognized the urgency in my voice instantly and wheeled from the coffee pot.

"I did a terrible thing!"

The pot slammed on the table.

"I lost Troubles!"

"How do you know?"

The solidarity of wedlock had cemented us into a single defense against disaster.

"I forgot about him when I got involved with the fence and he ran away. I yelled and yelled . . . "

"I'll talk to Buster alone. Bubbles may become unmanageable."

"Oh, honey! I feel so terrible. You know that girl and that dog . . . "

"No time for this sort of thing now. Get out there and keep Bubbles talking while I see what Buster wants to do. After this . . . "

He stopped, seeing the stricken look on my face. As he called Buster aside I stepped in front of Bubbles. In the light of the stables and their car's headlight I saw that she was carrying a huge globe filled with water. Inside it was a single gold fish.

"It's for my aquarium," said Bubbles proudly. "I'll put something over the top to keep Charlie Chan from getting it . . . did Troubles behave himself!" she asked, without pausing for breath between sentences.

"Oh, yes. Troubles didn't give me any trouble," I cried, making a hollow attempt at a joke.

"I knew he'd be okay if I left him in the cabin," said Bubbles.

We were nearing the cabin door. Frank and Buster were still in solemn conversation.

"Wait! Don't go in there!" I shouted. At the note of desperation in my tone Bubbles froze to attention. The water in the gold fish bowl sloshed dangerously.

"Bubbles! You must listen to me and not be angry!" I spoke so rapidly my words fell over each other. But I had started my confession and I couldn't stop. "I felt sorry for Troubles alone in the cabin and I let him out. He stayed with me all day. I watched him constantly. Then just at dark . . . he got away . . . I haven't been able to find him . . . "

The sound that came from Bubbles was shattering and inhuman. It was what the Irish call "keening." A horrible moaning between a shriek and a wail. It was blood curdling. And it grew louder.

The gold fish bowl fell from her grasp and I heard it shatter in a splash at our feet.

Buster and Frank arrived at the same instant that a growling and a scratching could be heard inside the cabin.

Buster threw open the door and as he flashed on the cabin lights, a furry form catapulted through the doorway, flinging itself into Bubbles' arms, yipping and whimpering.

"Troubles!"

The name burst from all of us.

The excited, happy dog flapped like a flounder, leaping from one to the other, barking high-pitched, laughing barks.

Bubbles laughed and cried.

I cried and laughed.

The two men stood speechless, grins bisecting their faces.

"How did he do it!" I cried. "Get back in the cabin?"

Buster pointed to the open window.

"But why didn't he answer when I called and called?"

"He doesn't, lots of times, when he gets tired of you calling him," said Buster.

I threw an arm around Buster and one around Bubbles.

"I'll never let Troubles loose again. I promise. And tomorrow I'm going to town to get you a new goldfish."

"Women!" snorted Frank, fairly spitting the word out. Buster scratched his head in wonderment.

Bubbles just laughed hysterically. It was a pretty scary sound but a welcome one after the keening. My flesh still crawls at the thought of it. What if Troubles hadn't come back? Suppose she had kept up the keening . . . It seems better not to explore that possibility.

The next time Bubbles went to visit Buster's people we made sure that Bubbles took Troubles with her.

I felt I owed Bubbles some sort of recompense for the near tragedy that I had almost brought into her life so I not only bought her a whole family of tropical fish for her aquarium but also some craft supplies.

If she liked to make things with her hands, it would be good therapy to let her, I reasoned. It might make her forget some of her grief for the baby, lessen her over-attachment to Troubles, and cause her to be just a mite gentler toward Buster.

Not knowing exactly which craft might bring about the greatest personality release and being something of a craft dabbler myself, I possibly overdid things. I bought Bubbles some leather belting and leather tooling implements, the makings of a hooked rug, some paint-by-number kits. one or two tile mosaics and a copper modeling set.

What I had never suspected was that Buster was the craft lover and Bubbles was really only interested in needlework.

From the day that the supplies arrived Buster closeted himself in the cabin and never came out to do any of the work on the ranch unless Frank forcibly dragged him out.

Then he would only work for a few minutes and just as soon as Frank was out of sight, he'd race to the cabin to hover for hours over a paint-by-number replica of The End of The Trail, or to crouch lovingly above a mosaic of Diana and the Hunt.

Bubbles meanwhile, like the Widow La Farge, knit constantly. What she was knitting we had no idea. She seemed to be working with the rug wool I had brought her but it did not appear to be a rug that she was fashioning. Whatever it was it grew longer and longer and wider and wider and went with her wherever she went.

You could glimpse her at any hour of the day, sitting beneath a live oak or nestled against a hay bale, with the voluminous folds of her knitting spread around her and Troubles asleep at her side.

Frank could be seen, meanwhile, hauling manure; currying the colts; longuing the yearlings and repairing the fence posts. But Buster's post was at his craft. He was in the midst of pressing an Indian profile in copper and frequently became so absorbed in his work that he didn't even stop for one of Bubbles' gourmet lunches of bread and milk.

I could sense that the barometer of Frank's wrath was reaching the boiling point and I knew who was the cause of it all. But how could I get Buster to give up his metal work or Bubbles to forsake her ubiquitous knitting!

One day I asked her what she was making.

She said it was a surprise for Frank but she'd tell me. A saddle blanket.

"Have you measured it on a horse?" I asked her, feeling, just from a glance, that it must be miles too big for one of the colts and seemed even to be growing too large for the expectant mares.

"I never thought of that," she said.

"There's only one horse gentle enough for us to measure it on," I said. "Big Mama. Let's try before you go any further so you'll have it the right size."

"Be sure that Frank doesn't see us."

"I'll make sure."

We slipped behind the barn; cross tied Big Mama and got out Bubbles' handiwork.

She had knit it of such bulky yarn and with such a close-knit stitch that it weighed almost more than the two of us together could raise from the ground. But struggling and straining, we managed to lift it over Big Mama's back. The old mare rolled her eyes and pawed the ground a bit but let it settle over her. And settle it did. From her poll it reached to her tail and hung down on either side clear to the ground. If it had been a coat of mail worn by a knight's horse it couldn't have more completely encompassed her.

"A saddle blanket is supposed to go under the saddle," I said to Bubbles.

"I guess I'll have to rip some out," she said, sadly.

We were very nearly trampled as we tried to remove Bubbles' creation from Big Mama because by now the mare was thoroughly terrified and convinced that Bubbles was weaving her shroud.

"I'll help you unravel," I said, seeing Bubbles' downcast mien.

We sat down on top of the hay and unravelled.

Three hours and eight wool skeins later we were still at it.

"I've got to go get dinner. You keep going!" I got a burlap bag and put the wound skeins in it.

"I don't think I'll make a saddle pad after all," said Bubbles. "I think I'll make a throw for Troubles to sleep on."

"I think that's a wonderful idea," I said and ran for the house.

As I passed the cabin Frank was pounding on it demanding that Buster come out and help him feed.

"Just a minute, Frank," called Buster, from within, "I'm in the midst of a tile tray now. I can't leave it till this glue sets."

I covered my ears against Frank's imprecations.

Why had I ever thought of craft work as therapy for the Glutzes?

Why?

It was the Griffiths who would soon need the therapy and where was it to come from?

Bubbles never cleaned the aquarium and all the tropical fish departed for a happier land.

She lost interest in her knitting and would sit for hours doing and re-doing her hair. (The flaming mane, I discovered, was a "piece" which she hung from the lamp pull in the cabin and every time I dropped in to see her I would recoil from it, imagining it was a fox swinging from the rafters.)

She was also becoming less and less cooperative about tying Troubles when strangers came to the ranch or when we were showing customers our horses.

Many of the people who come to the Bar None ostensibly shopping for a pleasure horse have only ridden one or two times in their lives, though they invariably tell us they are expert and experienced riders.

Frank knows the instant he sees someone attempt to bridle a horse or pick up the reins or lift a foot toward the stirrup exactly how long he has ridden and what manner of horse he can control. And we never let any dogs or pets, not even chickens, in the vicinity of mounting riders because we know that a wrong move on the part of rider or horse can easily cause a catastrophe.

Frank explained this to Bubbles and told her always to keep Troubles on the leash or tied whenever he was showing a prospect a horse. As she grew more and more lax about complying with this safety measure, it became my duty to track her and the dog down whenever visitors came to the ranch and to see that Troubles was kept in hand.

One Sunday just as Frank was about to help a very fearful and nervous prospect into the saddle, in an attempt to demonstrate the gentleness of one of the geldings, Troubles came bounding out of nowhere, chasing a butterfly and tore past the woman, causing the horse to rear.

Fortunately Frank was able to pull the horse down and keep the woman from losing her precarious balance and shoo Troubles away at the same time. But he was white with fright and anger at the realization of how narrowly serious consequences had been avoided.

Drawing me aside he said, "Tell Bubbles to tie up that dog and keep him tied and do it now or else pack up her things and get out."

I dragged Troubles with me to the cabin where Bubbles was just winding her bright red hair piece into python coils on top of her head.

"Bubbles!" I cried. And fright made me brusquer than I intended to be. "Frank and I are fed up with the way you let Troubles loose around here when we have people looking at the horses and you're either going to have to tie him the way you said you would when we agreed to let him stay here or you and Buster will have to leave."

I could see Bubbles' face turning purple to match her counterpane and the language that followed me out the door was a very deep blue. But I was just sufficiently upset to flounce out and slam the door after me.

Blinded by emotion I ran headlong into Buster, who came

by at the moment carrying his finished mosiac of The End of The Trail which he had just pasted on a tray back. As we collided the tray flew from his hand and crashed on the cement walk that leads to the cabin. Bits of horse, Indian, sky and mountain peppered the landscape.

"Oh Buster, I'm so sorry!" I cried, genuinely horrified that he should become the innocent victim of my anger. I sank to the ground trying to reclaim the scattered tiles.

The door behind me burst open and every kind of flotsam and jetsam that Bubbles could lay a hand on flew like flak around Buster and me. Her hair piece; her knitting needles; Troubles' toys; bits of seed crackers wrested from the parakeet's cage; her cowgirl boots; Buster's paintings and leather tools . . . we ducked and dodged, but I hadn't had as much practice at this sort of thing as Buster and I became a battered target.

My own anger was mounting now. Especially since Buster's metal mallet had struck me squarely in the torso, to be followed by a ball pein hammer to the mid-section.

"Get out of here both of you and get out now!" I cried and my voice was shaking as I was, with rage and indignation.

"Please, Mrs. Griffith," begged Buster. "Bubbles doesn't mean it. She just loses her temper sometimes but she really doesn't mean it."

"She's lost it for the last time on this ranch," I said. "Now pack. And get going!"

Out of the corner of my eye I could see the dismay on the face of the customer who had come to the Bar None looking for a pleasure horse.

I could also see Frank's look, and it undid me.

I stomped past him into the house and spent the next half hour picking paint, metal solder and tile cement off my ranch pants.

I went outside to find Frank and apologize for the scene I'd caused in front of his customer.

Bubbles was seated in the Glutzes' car with Troubles beside

her, her eyes straight ahead, her jaw set, the parakeet cage on her lap. Charlie Chan, the cat, reposed on the back seat next to the aquarium, which held stones but no fish.

Frank helped Buster strap the Glutzes' plastic suitcases to the top of the car. (All ranch help carry plastic suitcases, which is why the mere sight of a plastic suitcase is enough to give me a trauma to this day.)

It seemed incredible that what had appeared to be such a tender and permanent relationship between the Glutzes and the Griffiths should have been so violently and irrevocably dissolved in thirty minutes.

"Goodbye, Buster," I said, to let him know that my quarrel with Bubbles had not affected my feelings toward him. "I'm sorry about what happened today. I was very fond of Troubles. And Bubbles, too . . . "

Bubbles rolled the car window up on her side.

"Get in the house and stop acting as if you're sorry the Glutzes are leaving," Frank muttered in my ear. "If you hadn't fallen out with them I'd have had to throw him out anyway. I hired a ranch hand, not a Raphael."

An hour passed and we heard a tap at the back door. Frank opened it to behold Buster.

"Can't get the car to start, Mr. Griffith. I think maybe we need a push to get her off down the hill."

In stony silence Frank got out the Camino and pushed the Glutzes down the long grade that leads from the ranch.

"Have they gone?" I asked, when he finally returned, puffing at his pipe in a way that read "storm warning."

"They were rolling. That's all I know. And I'm glad to see the last of that dog, I can tell you. It's just a miracle he hasn't gotten us in some kind of a mess before now."

We settled down in silence before the fire and I felt terrible twinges of compassion for Bubbles, for Troubles, for poor Buster who must bear his albatross from job to job, and not just one albatross, either.

As I sat gnawing my fingers, pretending to read, we heard another tap on the back door.

Frank opened it to Buster, abject, apologetic, a sheepish grin on his face.

"Can't get the car under way, Mr. Griffith. I'm afraid you'll have to tow us back up so's I can work on her a little."

I avoided Frank's glance as he slipped his stockinged feet back into his work boots and followed Buster out the door.

Much later I heard the truck puff up the hill and then the sound of hammering and banging.

A little before midnight I brought coffee out which Buster and Frank accepted. Bubbles, asleep in the front seat, could not be aroused.

At two A.M. I saw Frank give the Glutzes car a push that started it down the grade.

He fell into bed exclaiming: "What a relief! The work was worth it to make sure they're really on their way!"

When we went out to feed at six the next morning, Buster was sitting on the back stoop.

"I'm sorry, Mr. Griffith, but she konked out again. I think you'll have to help me tow her back up . . . "

I shut the door quickly, not wanting to hear so much as the sound of Frank's thoughts.

For two days Frank alternately pushed and pulled Buster up and down the grade that runs through our valley.

In all that time I never saw Bubbles get out of the car, though I'm sure that there must have been times when she had to. She lived on crackers and fed crackers to Troubles, the parakeet and the cat. Buster was on his own. Whether he had any sort of nourishment or not, I had no way of knowing.

When he was on the repair half of the car cycle and working in our tool shed, I sneaked him some corn bread and coffee; enough to keep him going and Troubles, too. I never saw Bubbles accept any.

On the morning of the third day, with one last shove, the Glutzes left the Bar None forever.

The cabin was a shambles of craft supplies; half-finished paint-by-number masterpieces; flashy cowboy belts; sticky tile mosaics and parakeet seed. Bubbles had left so hurriedly, or rather, had tried to leave so hurriedly, that she left her hair piece behind her. It hung, like a bedraggled red fox, from the lamp pull. I took it in the house and hung it in the pantry where it serves as a constant reminder to me never again to lose my head at a time of hiring or firing.

13

Slinky, the Beloved Bum

Slinky is a bum.
And I love him.
Slinky is a panderer, philanderer, panhandler, fop.
And my best friend.
Slinky is a cat in the Marlboro Image: All Male.
As tom cats go Slinky is handsome. He boasts a sleek black
coat, neat white socks, an immaculate shirt front, and spanking
white whiskers.
With people Slinky is a mush.
With other toms Slinky is a tyrant.
It was not always so.
When Slinky was very young, itinerant tom cats used to
trounce him once a day and send him cowering to our back
door, cringing and licking his wounds.
Then something happened to Slinky's glands.
When the next stray tom came by, Slinky thwomped him.
And he's been Top Cat at the ranch ever since.
In his middle years Slinky has assumed the stance of a panther,
the jowls of a surrogate, and the character of a reprobate.
Slinky pretends to me that he is a Great White Hunter. After
he has badgered a bowl of milk out of me in the morning, he
slinks to the wash.

That is how he got his name: He never walks; he always slinks—a rippling, undulating, sexy glide designed to show off his quite superb musculature and flutter the hearts of sweet young girl cats.

After Slinky slinks to the wash, ostensibly for the purpose of catching one of the thousands of gophers and ground squirrels that have riddled the ranch till it looks like a sieve, Slinky goes to sleep.

Whole coveys of quail roam the hillsides.

Slinky ignores them.

The mice and the rats eat their way through half a ton of grain every year.

Slinky considers them beneath his notice.

When he feels impelled to dine on gophers, Slinky selects his dinner from a neighboring ranch.

He does not find our gophers to his taste.

Sometimes, just to show that he is on the ball, Slinky drags his catch home and deposits it on the back stoop; de-gutted and bleeding.

Or, he waits till I'm asleep in the hammock and jumps into my lap, bringing with him a decapitated lizard.

On other occasions Slinky has been known to bring gophers home inside his stomach.

He did this when our son, B.G., was still young and used to insist that Slinky sleep at the foot of his bed.

In the middle of the night we were awakened by B.G.'s loud howls.

Racing to his bedroom we discovered that Slinky had up-chucked a half-digested gopher in the center of the counterpane.

B.G. never invited Slinky to sleep with him after that.

Because Slinky is part Siamese he is talkative.

Whenever I iron beneath the live oak, or put my hair up in the shade of the sycamores, Slinky joins me and we have lengthy conversations.

He tells me about the gophers that got away.

And how nice the warm sun feels when he naps in the draw beside the dam.

He often mentions that the dew is very cold on his toes before sun-up.

And he complains bitterly about the boys on the next ranch. They are always setting out box traps in the hope of catching raccoons and skunks and other wild pets.

All they ever catch is Slinky.

"Why do you feed that bum of a cat when he can eat off the fat of the land?"

This is Frank, who, has a very low opinion of cats. I think it has something to do with the generic use of the word "cat" in connection with females.

"Slinky hunts all the time. I just like to give him a little milk once in a while."

"Slinky never hunts! And you know it! All the time you think he's hunting he's asleep in back of the pump house between the wall and the ivy where it's shady and cool and the flies can't get to him."

"Which just goes to prove he's a Smarty Cat!"

"Very funny! But it isn't so funny the way he lures female cats around here."

I had no retort. It was absolutely true. Tom cats are supposed to hunt down lady cats and stay away from home while they're courting them. But not Slinky. He brings them home with him.

We've had an endless succession of young brides and offspring to cope with. And all his mates turn out to be stringy, nervous types that get pregnant easily. Unfriendly, unappetizing cats that have five or six cats to a litter, preponderantly female.

And tom cats are supposed to devour their progeny, thereby helping to hold the cat population in check. But not Slinky. He is proud of his kits. Plays with them; lets them crawl all over him and pretend to nurse him. He even lets them cuff him and chew his ears and pounce on his tail.

In the spring, when Slinky's marital ventures sometimes get out of hand, we frequently find that he has brought home two or three wives and in no time they produce a round dozen of kittens.

Dearly would I love to share the charms of Slinky's delightful progeny with my neighbors by offering them pets from each litter.

But on the ranch we have a problem: No neighbors!

I won't take my cats to the Pound.

And I won't give them to the local Fire Department because they take them to the Pound.

So whenever I go in town I inquire among our friends if they would like a handsome, housebroken, trained-to-hunt ranch cat. And true friends always respond nobly and agree to take a cat or two. (I always urge my friends to take cats in pairs because they are happier that way.)

Of course they always ask if the cats are males.

And I always tell them they are.

And they always believe me.

It's the most amazing thing the way city folks can't tell the difference.

But one spring the litters were increasing and my circle of friends without cats diminishing. And I got pretty desperate.

Our son, B.G., at the time was weaving pot holders for the Boy Scout Fair. So I made a deal with him. I persuaded him to contribute some of his pot holders for a special promotion.

He and I went to the supermarket in town with a cute, be-ribboned basket filled with cute, be-ribboned kittens and a sign we'd painted reading:

FREE—SET OF POT HOLDERS WITH EVERY

FREE KITTEN . . . ALSO FREE CAN OF

CAT FOOD

ALL FREE

Wide-eyed moppets, innocent cat lovers every one, rushed to the basket, arms outstretched, faces wreathed in smiles, crying: "Oh, mommy, mommy, I want a kitten! It's free!"

"The pot holders and the cat food are free, too," my son would chirp, as I fixed a baleful eye upon him to make sure he read his lines properly.

Eager little hands reach out for an adorable kitten just as mommy bears down; eyes narrow, face furrowed by a ferocious frown.

"Don't go near those cats, Veronica! You know you're allergic to cat hair!"

"Come away from those dirty cats, Ravenswood, they carry disease!"

It was a most depressing experience.

Facing Frank with the be-ribboned basket full of be-ribboned kittens upon our return was even more depressing.

"If you don't get rid of those lousy cats, I'll . . . I'll . . . "

"You'll what?"

"I'll get rid of them myself!"

This was secretly what I hoped he would say.

Now I could close my eyes to the whole nefarious business and somehow in some way Frank would get rid of the kittens.

I don't know to this day how he does it, nor do I want to. But when new litters keep appearing while previous litters are only half grown; when the females out-number the males five to one, as they usually do; when as many as twelve or fifteen cats line up at the back door and race to get through it the minutes we open it, I am not in a bargaining position. The most I can do is sneak out one or two kittens that look most like Slinky.

I did this last spring and wound up with four identical Slinkies.

Every one had white socks, a white shirt front, a sleek black coat and white whiskers.

When they all grew to full stature it got pretty confusing.

Visitors could never tell the original from the facsimiles.

But I could. Because Slinky and I have a special rapport.

Apart from the headaches and the heartaches the cats cause us they also provide us with more free entertainment than television.

At the end of the day, when the kittens emerge from their day-long snooze all fresh and frisky, they put on a show that combines the talents of the Flying Wollendas, a Wrestling Tag Team Match, and Hyakawa's Tumblers all in one.

Up and down the trees they race, falling on us in a flurry of fur and claws if we're foolish enough to sit under them.

Chase their tails.

Spit and swat.

Now a leap into the air higher than Nazimova's.

We laugh at them until our sides ache. And even Frank has to admit if kittens just remained kittens and didn't turn into cats he might be able to tolerate them.

During the whole performance Slinky sits dozing on the sidelines; eyes green slits; white paws tucked neatly beneath him; whiskers twitching.

He is thinking what fun it is to be Top Cat at the ranch.

And to have all the wives he can handle.

And to have me to feed all the wives.

And their offspring.

Tomorrow, instead of hunting a gopher or tracking a squirrel or chasing a rat Slinky will squeeze through the doorway ahead of me and wind himself about my legs just as I am trying to carry a bowl full of slopping Jello to the refrigerator without spilling it. And I'll curse him and cuss him.

And then give him a bowl of milk.

14

Junior Was Strictly Umbilical

We had twenty-four head at the Bar None, as they say on television, not to mention manes and tails, and the work began to pile up on us.

I resisted calling the man at the state employment office but I couldn't resist sneaking a look at the "Situations Wanted" column of the Los Angeles Sunday *Times*. What a quick and painless way to get help! Why hadn't I thought of it sooner, I wondered, as I ploughed through sixteen pages of "Jobs Offered" to find less than half a column of "Situations Wanted."

I read the racy appeals for jobs in amazement!

"Adventurous male will do anything legitimate."

"Handsome, well-educated world traveler available as companion."

I caught glimpses of a new world, but found such vistas frightening.

A handsome, well-educated world traveler could scarcely be expected to consider the Bar None worthy of his itinerary.

But wait! The next entry seems tailor-made to our requirements.

"Reliable, sober man of integrity will consider honest employment."

Here was a prospect. A reliable and sober man, willing to

consider employment. There was an air of dignity and restraint about the phrasing that appealed to me.

I waited till Frank mounted Sir James and headed for the back pasture before dialing the number listed in the advertisement.

A woman answered. I almost hung up. Was this sober and reliable man married? The possibility hadn't occurred to me. Before I could put the phone down a female voice said: "This is Mrs. Blackwell speaking."

"I'm calling about an ad in the L.A. *Times* . . ."

"Oh, yes. Just a moment. Junior," she called, "it's for you."

"Loren Blackwell here," said a deep, refined voice at the other end of the line.

"Have you ever worked around horses, Mr. Blackwell?" I asked timorously.

This was the first question Frank would ask when I told him I'd found the perfect ranch hand.

A silence, quite possibly pregnant, was followed by a soft exclamation.

"Horses? Why, madam, I love horses. They've always had the keenest fascination for me. I've been interested in horses my entire life!"

The voice was so gracious and gentlemanly I couldn't wait to meet its owner.

"Well, we have a horse ranch and we need a hand and of course we always treat our hands just like a member of the family, but it's impossible to describe what our ranch is like. It's—well—sort of unique, you might say . . . But I know you'd love it and I wonder if you could come out to see us so you could see if you'd like to work here . . ."

"Why I believe I could do that," he murmured agreeably. "Just a moment . . . Mother!" he called, to someone nearby "come here and take down the directions to get to this lady's ranch."

The woman who had initially answered the phone returned to the wire.

"Would Loren have a good home with you people?" she asked, before I could say anything. "Are you a nice, clean living family?"

"I . . . I think so," I said uncertainly. The question was open to various interpretations. "We don't drink or have wild parties and I guess you'd say we're hard working . . . "

"Junior doesn't drink. He's clean living," she said decisively. "I wouldn't want him with any family that wasn't clean living."

"Maybe you'd better come with him and see for yourself what sort of family we are," I offered, and gave her the directions to the ranch.

"I'll bring Junior out this afternoon," she said. "What'd you say your name is?"

"Griffith. Rubye and Frank Griffith."

"We knew some Griffiths back in Tennessee where we came from was good clean livers," said Mrs. Blackwell. Without further comment she hung up the phone.

"There's a man coming out to see us this afternoon about a job," I told Frank when I figured the Blackwells must be well on their way to the Bar None.

Storm signals: Brows lowered; pipe put-putting.

"A single man!" I cried instantly, feeling certain the woman I spoke to must be Junior's mother.

"You called the state employment office!" roared Frank.

"I did not! I answered an ad in the *Times*."

"O Lord!" a groan dragged from the nether regions.

"This man is real refined. He doesn't drink and he loves horses!"

"Does he know how to work with horses?"

"That was the first question I asked him! He said he's absolutely fascinated by horses, in fact they've been his chief interest most of his life!"

As I said this I dodged behind some hay bales, ostensibly searching for eggs. I found one, still nicely warm, and slipped around the hay to head for the house.

I put the egg in the egg basket I keep in the pantry and just then I heard a car in the drive. I ran out to get a look at it. It wasn't a bad car. Though of fairly ancient vintage, it was shiny and had a cared-for look. The sort of look you'd expect a car to have that belonged to a little old lady in Altadena, which is where the Blackwells hailed from.

And, remarkably enough, a little old lady was in the driver's seat and at her side sat a stalwart white-haired gentleman.

I took a better look.

Could this be Junior? If it was I'd better head for the hills because Frank was coming toward the car.

With relief I noticed another man emerging from the back of the car.

"Loren Blackwell," he announced, extending a damp, limp hand. He was tall, slender, rather good-looking in a tired, tremulous way, and boasted a shock of iron-grey hair.

He introduced the white-haired couple as his mother and stepfather.

Mrs. Blackwell was a raw-boned, Grant Wood kind of woman, dressed in a shapeless mother hubbard, her hair pulled back in a haphazard knot. Her handshake was not at all limp; it was a bone crusher.

Mr. Blackwell was heavy-set and twinkly. He gave the impression of knowing a secret that kept him highly amused.

Frank and Junior walked off to tour the ranch and I settled Mr. and Mrs. Blackwell beneath a live oak tree and rushed out iced tea and thick wedges of chocolate cake, which, with canny foresight, I had just whisked from the oven.

Mr. Blackwell chatted pleasantly of the beauty of our hill country; the changes that had taken place in California over the past fifty years and the likelihood of a wet winter.

Mrs. Blackwell maintained a fretful silence which was suddenly and inexplicably shattered by a violent outburst of tears, accompanied by racking sobs.

I sprang to my feet.

"Is your wife ill?" I asked Mr. Blackwell.

"No. She ain't ill," he said calmly and continued to munch his chocolate cake. Rivers of tears slid down Mrs. Blackwell's wrinkled cheeks which Mr. Blackwell observed with the detachment of a person watching television.

I was about to yell to Frank when Mrs. Blackwell managed to control her sobs sufficiently to gasp: "You will take good care of my baby, won't you?"

Was this another Bubbles with a poor lost baby, mourned for half a century, I wondered? Mrs. Blackwell looked at least seventy.

"My Junior!" she cried. "He's such a good boy. He can't help it if life's been unkind to him."

Mr. Blackwell gave a snort that nearly blew the cake off his plate.

Mrs. Blackwell continued to sob. When she could control herself she said, between sniffles: "Junior's only fifty-four. It's tough for a young fellow his age to get a job."

I must have looked my astonishment because Mr. Blackwell gave a mighty guffaw.

"I hope . . . Junior . . . knows something about horses. If he doesn't he may get hurt," I said. I almost choked on the word "Junior."

"Why Junior's made a study of horses all his life!" cried Mrs. Blackwell.

"Blasted idiot doesn't know a damned thing about horses or anything else," said a voice I felt certain must have come from Mr. Blackwell, but when I glanced at him he was staring at his plate and I couldn't be sure he had spoken.

"You will be good to my boy, won't you!" begged Mrs. Blackwell. "Junior's so sensitive. "Where is he going to stay?" she asked suddenly.

I pointed to the cabin, not trusting myself to speak.

"I brought his things with me. If it's all right with you I'll put them in his room," she offered.

"Don't you think we'd better find out if . . . Junior . . . has decided to stay at the Bar None?" I asked uncertainly.

"If he hasn't decided I have!" My eyes flew to Mr. Blackwell again. He was staring at his cake with such an innocent expression I wondered, once again, if he had spoken.

"Will you please show me where Junior will sleep?" asked Mrs. Blackwell querulously.

I lead her to the cabin, now vacant and characterless. What new ectoplasmic aura was about to be impressed upon it, I wondered.

Mrs. Blackwell looked about her critically.

"It's not very big but I guess it will have to do," she sighed. She punched the mattress with her fist. "Junior's used to a Beautyrest," she said.

It seemed best not to comment.

Mrs. Blackwell shambled to the car and returned with her arms full of exquisite hand-tailored shirts; magnificent hand knit sweaters; rows of handsomely ironed slacks and an assortment of sleeping garments.

She stretched them out on the bed and I passed them to her as she hung them in the tiny closet.

She made two more trips to the car, returning each time with tremendous cardboard boxes.

Pushing and pulling as a team we managed to get them into Junior's boudoir.

One box contained more than a dozen pairs of shoes all neatly polished; the other held underwear, handkerchiefs, and socks, all meticuously arranged and spanking white as a Tide ad.

Mr. Blackwell looked up from his cake occasionally as his wife and I struggled with Junior's belongings, but he did not offer any help.

As the last of the clothing was transferred from the car to the cabin Frank and Junior reappeared and I could tell from the expression on Frank's face that he had decided to give

Junior a trial. Shoveling manure can get mighty monotonous when you shovel three or four hours a day seven days a week and we had been without help quite a while—ever since the departure of Bubbles and Buster.

"I think I could learn to like it here, Mother," said Junior, in the tone of a five-year-old who has just agreed to give kindergarten a try.

"I hope you understand horses, Blackwell," said Frank.

"Oh I've studied horses all my life," said Junior grandly.

Mrs. Blackwell shielded her mouth with her hand and spoke in a crackling whisper to Junior through her dentures.

"This seems to be a decent place and these seem to be decent, clean living people. Do try to make the best of it, dear boy," she said tenderly.

"He damned well better, sick as I am of the sight of him!"

Again my eyes flew to Mr. Blackwell. Had he spoken? No one else could have made the comment. But his gaze rested on his cake, his face remained expressionless.

I continued to watch him and presently he looked up and the barest twinkle flashed in his crinkled blue eyes.

I looked away to study Junior's ensemble as he bade his mother goodbye.

He wore slacks and a matching sweater of avocado green. Beneath the sweater I glimpsed a sage green shirt and a narrow, carefully knotted tie.

I looked down at my own faded jeans. They were rump-sprung and splattered with colt slobber. Bits of manure clung lovingly to my lady Wellingtons.

Junior's fashionable apparel set a frightfuly high standard for us.

I wondered if we'd be able to live up to it.

Mrs. Blackwell had thrown her arms around Junior and was tenderly brushing the hair back from his brow. She had to stand on tiptoe to do it. "I'll write every day and I'll call, too, and next week end I'll be up with clean things for you," she said. "Just throw your dirty clothes in a box and I'll take them home and launder them for you."

Suddenly her face broke apart and sobs rattled her gaunt, shapeless body.

She strained Junior to her fiercely and cried out tearfully: "Oh, poor boy! Poor boy!"

Mr. Blackwell belched.

"Mother always gets a little upset when we have to be apart," said Junior. He brushed tears from his eyes.

I looked at Frank but looked away quickly.

Junior escorted his mother to the car and told her he would write regularly and keep in touch by phone.

Mr. Blackwell gave me a pinch on the fanny as he walked by and whispered in my ear: "Don't let Junior get kicked by any wild horses!" He winked and his large frame shook with suppressed laughter.

The car eased out of sight and Junior was ours.

Frank had sprinted for the house and I was left alone with our hand.

"Do you think your mother is in fit condition to drive?" I asked him.

"Oh yes. Mother's really a remarkable woman. She's a tailor, you know. Has been for over fifty years. My step dad retired long ago, but not mother. She still sews for some of the finest men's stores in Los Angeles." (This explained Junior's elegant wardrobe.) "Mother'll be seventy-five next year and she says she's going to quit work. But I doubt it. A remarkable woman," he repeated. "Sometimes a little too demonstrative."

That was certainly an understatement!

"Well, I guess you'll want to bunk down," I said. "There's plenty of food in the cabin so go right ahead and fix yourself something to eat."

Junior's well-bred face fell.

"You mean I have to cook for myself?" he asked tremulously.

It was a moment of decision. I could wind up as I always did

—docile and defeated—or I could play it tough. With Junior it suddenly seemed as if it might be real jolly to play it tough.

"That's right. You have to cook your own meals," I said in what I hoped would seem a decisive tone.

"And do I have to live all by myself in that cabin?" asked Junior.

I knew what Mother Blackwell would do at a time like this. I did just the opposite. "That's right!" I said. Junior recognized firmness when he met it. Pouting and with trembling lip he retired to his cabin.

It may be said of Junior that in truth he was a horse lover. He spent all his time figuring out which horses would win at the track. And when he called Mother Blackwell it was to pass along his findings to her, as much as to assuage her lonely mother's heart with the sound of his voice.

Junior's great love for the species Equinus did not, however, extend to those members of it not yet ready to compete at Santa Anita. When it came time to muck stalls he put on hip boots, gauntlet gloves, wound a scarf around his nose and drew a smart beret over his hair. In this garb he delicately removed the surface droppings but he would never really get down to bedrock.

It became apparent at the outset that Junior Blackwell would go down in history as another of Rubye's follies. But we didn't have any other help (old refrain). The optimist at the state employment office didn't have any either, so we had to put up with Junior. And he really did lend tone to the place. We'd never had anyone so CLEAN before. And, in the rare intervals when he wasn't absorbed in the scratch sheets that mother mailed him daily, Junior did try to curry the horses.

Of course he knew nothing about the need for cross tying a horse before grooming it; he had never lead a horse and so was in constant danger of having one walk on him. He didn't know that he should turn their rumps away from him before letting them loose at pasture and so invited a kick every time they took off.

Junior's idea of currying was to run a brush over the horse as daintily as if he were powdering a baby's bottom. This feather light touch made the horses skittish because it tickled them, so again he was in danger of being kicked.

But Junior had not lied about one thing. He was of good background—he behaved always with the courtesy and formality of an Englishman in the presence of royalty. He was always smoothshaven, immaculate, even his fingernails were clean. It was rather a refreshing change.

Mrs. Blackwell returned at the end of Junior's first week with clean clothes, as promised. She gathered up the dirty ones (Junior changed his wardrobe two or three times a day) and brought from the car writing paper, tins of cookies, scratch sheets, and a room deodorant. She commiserated with Junior at not having selected any winners the past week and handed him twenty dollars as a sop to his grief.

Mr. Blackwell remained in the car and I went over to chat with him.

"How's Joy Boy doing?" he asked with his splintery twinkle.

"As well as may be expected," I answered.

"I've had forty-five years of this," he said. "That's how long I've been married to his mother. Don't think I could stand another forty-five."

I laughed but my laughter was hollow.

"When he got married I thought the cord might be severed."

"You mean Junior's married!"

"Married and the father of eight children!"

If I hadn't been blessed with an exceptionally robust physique I think I'd have fainted.

"Close your mouth," said Mr. Blackwell. "You'll only catch flies that way!"

With an effort I managed to close it.

"Where are they? His wife and children?"

"Down in Mississippi, the last place he got stranded. His mother supports them. That's why she's still working."

At that moment the arrival of Mrs. Blackwell prevented further family revelations and for this I was grateful.

Sobs tore through her shapeless body. Tears spattered down her tired, lined face.

She managed a rainbow smile through them.

"Take good care of my boy," she begged. "He's awfully lonesome there alone in that cabin. He'd hoped to be part of the family when he came here. He's not used to being treated like a servant. It would cheer him up a lot if you could see he spent his evenings with you people. Junior's good company. He's been everywhere!"

"Going from one job to another," Mr. Blackwell noted dourly.

"You don't understand Junior! You've never understood him! How could you possibly, you're so . . . so insensitive!"

Mr. Blackwell belched heartily, and all at once I realized that he employed belching as a form of sub-vocal commentary by means of which he was able to express his feelings without over-stimulating Mrs. Blackwell's lachrymal glands.

Whereas formerly I had pitied him, I now found myself looking at him with the greatest admiration.

In the middle of his second week at the Bar None Junior had a tantrum. He didn't lie down on the floor and hold his breath; he simply hung up on his mother in the middle of a phone conversation; then he flounced into the ranch kitchen white-lipped.

"Mother makes me so angry!" he cried and stomped his well shod foot petulantly.

Frank and I said nothing.

"She knows I need a car to get to the races on my day off and she won't advance me the money to buy one."

Frank and I still said nothing. We sensed an impending "touch," or at the least, a request for a salary advance.

"If you'd let me borrow your ranch truck I could drive over to mother's and . . ."

"I don't loan my car to anyone," said Frank.

"Surely you know that you can trust me to return it safely," said Junior with a pout.

"Sorry. That's the way it is," said Frank in his no-nonsense tone.

Junior stalked out of the kitchen with his nose in the air.

He did the chores as usual, enveloped in face mask, gauntlet gloves, etc., and just as we were sitting down to supper he reappeared at the kitchen door.

"I'd like my pay. Whatever is due me," he said abruptly.

Without a word Frank arose and counted out the money to him.

"I'm sorry to leave this way but I feel this job was not as represented," he remarked loftily.

"In what way?" asked Frank. It amazed me that he was able to control his temper since I felt my own temperature rising.

"I expected to become part of the family in a respectable home and to enjoy human companionship, not to be thrust by myself in help's quarters."

"If my wife gave you that impression it is because she is a writer and given to exaggeration," said Frank, looking at me steadily in the hope of enjoying my reaction.

Refusing to let him have his fun, I simply smiled ever so sweetly.

"There's no need to worry about me getting home."

"You mean you have transportation?"

"I'll phone mother up at the corners. She'll come and get me!"

"Oh no!" I thought. "Not drag that poor old woman out of bed and make her drive over a hundred miles . . ." I could imagine Mr. Blackwell when the call came. I felt certain he would summon up a particularly robust burp to express his secret opinion of Junior and Mother Blackwell.

"I've left my clothes in the closets in the cabin. Mother will come for them over the weekend. Thank you for your hospitality." This last was spoken with icy innuendo. And Loren Blackwell walked out of our life.

In looking back on our experiences with the many poor lost souls who have temporarily found a haven with us, I have always felt that Junior and Mother Blackwell taught me one of life's most valuable lessons.

When our son joined the Navy and turned his back on home and suddenly attempted to break off all parental ties and make it on his own, I was able to release him gladly, completely, and gratefully, turning him over completely to God's care.

What made it possible, in fact, imperative for me to do this?

A solemn vow I made to Frank and to myself the night Junior took off.

I said at the time, and I meant it: "Frank, if I ever give the slightest indication of becoming an umblical mother like Mrs. Blackwell; if I ever encourage B.G. to cling to me or depend on me or become emotionally attached to me, I want you to get out the shotgun and take careful aim and let me have it—right between the eyes!"

15

The Hawk Takes a Chance on Romance

How pleasant it is to be help-less, I thought, as I sat on my favorite knoll overlooking the Bar None. The mares strolled peacefully through the pastures, each with a colt at her side.

A splash of silver sound fell through the sun-bright air, marking the flight of a meadowlark.

The mares had all been bred back; we had a new crop of foals in the making. Our generous-hearted neighbor, Ronald Reagan, had invited us to breed our mares to his permanently registered Appaloosa stud, Hank's Spotted Brave, without charge. If we got Appaloosa, fine. If we didn't, at least we could be sure of beautiful, well-conformed colts.

It was a time of fecund tranquility at the Bar None.

And why were things so tranquil?

Because the help's cabin was empty. And, in our help-lessness, Frank and I found time to revel in our privacy, our horses, and each other.

Then the work started to get ahead of us. And, inevitably, the cry of "Help!" went out to our friendly friend at the state employment office. He responded to it with his customary

171

good will and optimism. This time he had THE ranch hand for us: conscientious, reliable, kind to man and beast.

As usual I believed him.

As usual Frank didn't.

But Frank's face brightened when the Hawk descended upon us.

Hawk Ronson was no little hawk. He stood six-foot-three, minus his cowboy boots, and his shoulders would just about go through a door. He had a friendly, ingenuous face that looked upon the human comedy with more amusement than rancor.

Hawk's voice was not little either. He either bellowed or boomed. Hawk told us he'd been in an accident when he was young and as a result he had injured his hip. This caused him to walk with a huge, hopping limp. Hawk could cover ground faster at a limp than a gaited horse could at the rack. And he wasn't shy of work.

This may have explained why Hawk and Frank hit it off instantly, and established a robust, man-to-man relationship from which I was pointedly excluded.

This suited me perfectly.

I'd suffered enough from emotional entanglements with Felice, Bubbles, and Junior and had no desire to sink without a trace in Hawk's problems.

I decided to enjoy what I realize now is our "grace period" —the halcyon time when a new hand is not sufficiently entrenched to reveal the many hidden facets of his personality.

"I guess you noticed Hawk hasn't any teeth," observed Frank as he poured a bag of oats in the feed bin. He added a bag of bran and I stirred the mixture with a shovel.

"Yes I noticed." When Hawk smiled he displayed only hard polished, toothless pink gums.

"I thought maybe you'd like to stake him to dentures. Maybe you could find the same dentist that outfitted Maria . . ."

"Very funny. You should be writing situation comedy."

Frank chuckled as he watched Hawk lift a three-wire hundred and eighty pound bale of hay over his head and walk it to the pick-up.

"There's the first worker we've ever had at the ranch," Frank said happily.

The next day was Hawk's day off, and he didn't come back. "I guess I'd better call the state employment office," I said about three-thirty the following day. "You know how long it takes them to find anyone . . ."

Just then the phone rang and it was Hawk. He told Frank he'd come to in a bar about a hundred miles from the ranch and had no money left. As soon as he could bum a ride to the Bar None, he'd be home.

Hawk showed up the following morning, grubby, unshaven, bleary-eyed and abject.

Without stopping to wash or change his clothes he went right to work and didn't stop working for the rest of the day.

Frank made no reference to his indiscretion.

After that, every time Hawk took a day off, he followed the same pattern.

Just when we were ready to give him up altogether, he would come flailing down the lane, hopping on his good leg and swinging his game leg in block-long strides.

Without a word he'd go right to work and do the work of three.

Frank never referred to Hawk's backslidings or made any comment about his drinking since Hawk never drank at the ranch.

He worked all week without a let-up; but as the time for his big fling approached he became short-tempered and twitchy and complained about everything till we really were glad to see him go. While under the influence Hawk apparently released all his hostilities and tensions for he would return dispirited, but compliant and eager for work.

Although Hawk was obviously an alcoholic he was truly a reliable and conscientious worker; but in addition to his drinking Hawk had one other vice: an insatiable, gargantuan appetite!

Several years of cooking for ranch hands has accustomed me to the fact that men who work outdoors at rugged labor just naturally go for second and even third helpings. But no one I've ever seen could stow away food the way Hawk could.

If he had agreed to cook for himself I wouldn't have minded it. But Hawk made it clear the day Frank hired him that he couldn't cook worth a nickel and he'd sure like to have me dish up chow for him.

It seemed a simple enough request—until I discovered that Hawk's stomach had no bottom.

For breakfast he regularly consumed eight fried eggs, four slices of buttered toast (or biscuits or cornbread if available); then he'd tackle a big bowl of hot cereal; polish off two stacks of pancakes and a quart of milk, and wind up with sausage or ham or some other breakfast meat.

By mid-morning Hawk usually downed another quart of milk and several slices of bread. (He never took time to add butter.)

Lunch and supper were in proportion to his dainty breakfast. He devoured meat and potatoes, a vegetable, hot bread and dessert and, of course, another quart of milk. But it was after supper, while watching television in the cabin, that Hawk really started eating. He had his own larder, which we kept stocked with family size cans of tuna and gallon jars of mayonnaise and several loaves of bread.

From the seven o'clock news through the late, late show, a line-up of entertainment which Hawk watched regularly, he frequently ate his way through four of the giant cans of tuna; two loaves of bread and another quart of milk.

Still he would come to the breakfast table ravenous as ever, ready to fall to once more.

I once remarked to Hawk that he should be happy to be able to eat as much as he did without having to worry about his figure.

"But then," I added politely, "you're such a big man I suppose it's only natural for you to require a lot of fuel."

"Shucks, ma'am," laughed Hawk, with one of the booming guffaws that sounded like boulders shaking loose in the canyon. "I'm just a little squirt compared to my brother."

I must have looked disbelieving for Hawk laughed louder, causing the chickens to scatter in consternation and the dog to give a threatening growl.

"I only weigh two hundred and sixty and I'm only six foot three," he said modestly. Then he whipped a crumpled snapshot out of a crumbling wallet and thrust it at me. "See there. That there's my big brother, Tim. We set out to be identical twins, only Tim overshot me. He growed to be seven feet tall and he weighs over three hundred. No fat on him, neither."

I looked at the snapshot in awe. Sure enough there stood the Hawk next to a king-size replica of himself. The replica towered above him and was, in very truth, a hard muscled giant without an once of fat on him.

"Where's your twin now, Hawk?" I asked, hoping he would be far away so that I would never have to feed him.

"Tim's back East. He's a miner," said Hawk proudly. He carefully tucked the crumpled snapshot back in his wallet. I could see why it was so nearly in shreds. Hawk liked to show off his twin brother and why not? Not every twin could boast such a big, BIG, BIG brother.

Tim must really haul some coal, I thought. I'd sure hate to have to feed him. Aren't we lucky to have the runt of the litter.

Hawk fancied himself quite a horseman. But he was so loud in his speech and his movements were so jerky that he kept the horses in a state of perpetual shock.

He wanted to ride so earnestly that Frank let him have Sir James and he'd spring aboard Sir James from the ground, bareback, and fling his game leg over the horse's back, like Chester in Gun Smoke. Then he'd go wahooing through the pasture with the intention of rounding up the colts.

The yearlings would hightail it for the hills as soon as they heard Hawk's first wahoo, raising a mushroom of dust behind them. Hawk would circle them for a while, booming and bellowing, then return empty-handed.

Frank would rattle the feed bin and whistle and the colts would hightail it back to stand at the gate waiting for Frank to catch them.

"Ornery little critters! I'll catch 'em next time," roared Hawk, laughing good naturedly and baring his shining pink gums. But never once did he get within mare's length of them.

After he'd been with us about two months Frank noticed that Hawk had great difficulty getting around. His limp was becoming more and more noticeable and sometimes we suspected that he was actually in pain.

Hawk finally admitted that his leg was having one of its annual flare-ups and he'd have to go to the hospital to have it attended to as he had for the past fifteen years.

"How long do you think you'll be laid up?" asked Frank.

"About a month or six weeks."

"Okay. We'll do the work ourselves and keep your job for you till you get well."

The next day Frank took Hawk to the hospital and we settled down to a period of help-lessness until Hawk should return.

Within a week the doctor phoned Frank to explain that there was not room in the hospital for Hawk to stay while he recovered from his operation. Since there was really no further medical treatment required, simply a period of convalescence, the doctor released Hawk from the hospital. He was on his way to the ranch in an ambulance and the doctor suggested we take good care of him until he was strong enough to work.

Naturally we never once thought of doing anything but nursing the Hawk back to health.

He came home, a wan, pale giant, bearded and reduced to pathetic meekness by the sights and sounds of hospital life.

How happy he was to see us. How grateful for his cabin. How delighted with the sweet smell of the hay, the rompings of the colts, the blazing blue of our California sky, and the sight of the mountains, just at daybreak, brushed with the butter of sunshine.

He could do nothing, nor would we let him. But he sat in the sun, with the crutch provided by the hospital at his side, and cleaned and polished tack and mended rope and whistled and hummed and it made us happy just to see him getting all his old spunk back. And we knew that the Hawk had recovered when he let out a roaring guffaw that sent all the mares flying for the hills with their tails up and manes flying like sea spume.

Hawk in convalescence consumed twice as much food as Hawk in the bloom of health for he had nothing to do now but eat.

Six-egg egg-nogs, wrapped in quarts of milk, slipped out of sight without a trace.

I made so many trips back and forth to the cabin bearing ten-egg omelets and thick slabs of roast beef that finally I told Frank I thought we should move the Hawk into the guest room till he recovered, since it would make so much less work for all of us.

Hawk ensconced in the guest room with television blaring from seven in the morning till the wee small hours was pretty scarring to the psyche, I'll admit.

But it was still easier than traipsing back and forth to the cabin.

We gave him cigarettes. He piled up stubs in the ash trays and of course how could he be expected to empty them?

We asked him if there was anything he might like to read,

hoping thus to distract him for a while from the television.

He asked for comic books.

We brought him dozens and dozens of comic books. He read them as fast as we brought them to him. To the accompaniment of the television.

His wound had to be dressed every day and this Frank did.

His clothes and his bedding had to be kept clean and this I did.

One day I got the wild idea if Hawk were only married his wife could be taking care of him. The mere thought of a woman having to feed the brute and look after him seemed like an awfully dirty trick to play on any woman. But if someone could love him . . .

"Hawk, how is it you aren't married?" I asked him, as he sat polishing boots beneath the live oak tree.

He jumped as if a diamond back had come out of the boot he was cleaning.

"You'll never get me to marry . . . again," he snorted. The snort was so big it sent three kittens scurrying up the tree over his head.

I watched his hands as they carefully followed the tooling on Frank's boot. They were so large that the boot, cradled in them, looked no larger than a baby's bootee.

"Oh did you have a bad experience, Hawk?" I asked sympathetically, wishing I'd never touched on a subject so fraught with pain for him.

"You be the judge, ma'am. My woman up and left me and sold all the furniture we had without telling me and took the money with her and I ain't never been able to find her. You be the judge."

"I judge you got the wrong woman, Hawk. The world's full of a whole lot of better ones."

"I doubt that largely," said Hawk.

"It's true, Hawk. You'd make some woman a fine husband. And if you were married it would help you to give up drinking.

I know you do want to give it up," I said boldly. I had never mentioned the subject of drinking to Hawk, nor had Frank. But we both felt that he was miserable because of his enslavement to alcohol and wished heartily he could break the vicious habit.

"Yes, ma'am. I do." he said in the closest he could come to a whisper. It was still louder than most conversational tones. "But I get lonely and then . . ."

"I know. And if you were married you wouldn't get so lonely. You really should think about it."

"I've thought about it. When I'm sober. But I don't know. I get to thinking of that woman and my furniture and . . ."

"You mustn't look back, Hawk. That isn't good. How long ago did your first wife make off with your furniture?"

Hawk took plenty of time to do a little mental figuring. At length he came up with the answer. "Sixteen years, ma'am."

"Oh, Hawk! Really. You mustn't let something that happened sixteen years ago embitter you. Make a new life for yourself with a good woman. You've got so many years ahead of you. You can have a happy marriage."

"Maybe you're right," said Hawk. And as I walked away I saw him look off to the mountains, his big face furrowed by thoughtfulness.

The sight of Hawk in cogitation brought a lump to my throat. I decided not to say a word to Frank about our talk. Frank thinks all women are incurable matchmakers.

But I was getting awfully tired of cooking for Hawk.

At the end of six weeks Hawk was getting around without crutches and Frank decided by the next week end he could resume his duties at the ranch.

But first Hawk wanted to take a couple of days off and visit his relatives in a nearby town.

As he took off in the station wagon of a neighbor who had kindly offered to give him a lift to the bus depot, his hair slicked down, his beard shaved off, and his brand new jeans and boots, gleaming in the sunlight, I wondered if we would ever see Hawk again.

All this time away from civilization . . . would he go off the deep end for good, in spite of our little discussion?

He surprised us both by coming home on time and sober.

He remained clean shaven and smiling the whole week and took off again the following weekend and again returned on time and sober.

"Something funny about Hawk," said Frank finally. "He isn't hitting the bottle on his day off. Do you think maybe he's really trying to get away from the stuff."

"I think maybe he's found a good influence in his life," I said eagerly. "I think he's in love!"

"Omigawd!" gulped Frank, almost swallowing his pipe, which he happened at the time to be lighting.

"Well he needn't bring any woman around this place. No more couples at the Bar None. Not after Bubbles and Buster. Why if I thought for a minute that he thought for a minute . . ."

"Honey, don't you see this would be different? If Hawk got himself a nice sensible wife she could cook for him and clean house for me and he wouldn't get lonely and that means he'd stay here and you know you like him."

Frank gave me the look. The look of horror. The look he gets when it suddenly begins to dawn on him that I am conniving. I suddenly remembered I had something to do to the horses. I ran all the way to the pasture gate. And then I stood there. Wouldn't anything be worth not having to cook for Hawk? I wondered.

Frank, who can be as subtle as a bulldozer if he really puts his mind to it, looked at Hawk, one morning, at breakfast and said, without even a preamble:

"Hawk! Are you planning to get married!"

Hawk, who was balancing a sixth egg on his fork, preparatory to swallowing it, dropped the egg in his oatmeal, but undisturbed, swirled it in the oatmeal and swallowed two or three spoonsful of the mixture before he replied. Then he looked Frank directly in the eye and said, as if he were taking an oath for office: "So help me, God, Mr. Griffith, may I be struck down this instant, if I planned to do a dumb thing like that."

Frank relaxed and laughed out loud.

"Well now that sounds more like it," said he approvingly.

I looked at Hawk with my mouth open. Was that all the impression my uplifting and inspirational discussion had on him?

"I'm through with women and you can say amen to that, by golly. One woman made a fool of a man is enough. I ain't about to try for it again, no I ain't!"

"Well I'm sure glad to hear that," said Frank. "Cause we don't want any couples working for us. So if you figure on staying here you'd better figure on staying single."

"No woman on earth gonna get her hooks into me," smiled Hawk, lapping up the last of the oatmeal and reaching out for the pancakes.

I flounced out of the kitchen.

"Men! Deceitful cads every one of them. It'd be a long time before I wasted any more time talking to Hawk!" This was spoken quite privately, to myself.

Hawk was all slicked up, dressed in his town clothes and with his face clean shaven, grinning his toothless grin and cracking his huge hands together so that the knuckles snapped, when the fire broke out.

It was about three miles north of the ranch with a good wind behind it and heading straight for the hay.

In seconds I was on the line to the fire department.

"What's the good word, Ella?" I asked the dispatcher. "This is the Bar None."

"It's two ranches west of you. If the wind stays at present

velocity, look for trouble. Better wet your hay. We've got equipment on the way!"

Frank and I worked like automatons, dragging out hose, hooking the lengths together, moving the insecticides and other inflammables away from the stables, corralling the stock. We've been through three near-disaster fires at the Bar None and we don't panic easily. We know what we have to do and we do it and leave the rest to God.

We called orders to Hawk, now and then, asking him to haul a length of hose or move some bales of hay; and though he did whatever we asked him to do, we could sense that he just wasn't with it. His gaze rested on the horizon but not in the direction where black smoke rose threateningly.

He seemed more concerned about keeping his clothes from getting soiled than he was in saving the ranch.

There was about an hour left till dusk and we knew if the fire didn't get under control by then we'd have a long night of terror ahead of us.

"I hope you don't think you're going in town tonight, Hawk," Frank said at last, as Hawk continued to look at his watch every few minutes." We'll need all the help we can get here if this turns into the real thing."

"I ain't aimin' to pull out whilst the fire's ragin'," said Hawk impatiently. "But I gotta get my hair cut tonight and no mistake!"

Frank and I stared at him in astonishment. The ranch was threatened by dissolution and Hawk was afraid he might miss having his hair cut!

The language that poured from Frank's lips was hotter than the blaze of the fire.

"You get busy with that hose and wet down the stable roof or you won't have a head left to cut hair off!"

Hawk grabbed the hose, turned it on the stables and said nothing.

Forty minutes later the wind shifted and the black column

of smoke at first wavered, then lightened and ever so slowly diminished till we could no longer see it.

A short while after the phone rang.

I answered it on the extension in the tack room.

"That was the fire department," I told Frank. "We're in the clear. They said they'll be on guard all night."

"Can I go now?" cried Hawk, before the words were out of my mouth.

"Yes, you can go!" snapped Frank.

Hawk sprinted down the lane like a charging moose, arms flailing, his huge feet sending up clouds of dust.

"I never saw a man wanted a haircut that badly," muttered Frank.

"He should remember what happened to Samson," I said as we set about putting the colts back in the corrals and letting the mares out to pasture.

If I had only known that my words were prophetic!

Hawk's uncle frequently brought him back to the ranch in a camper after his day off. The uncle would whirl in the lane and roar out again, barely slowing enough to let Hawk alight. We had grown accustomed to this routine and when the camper rolled in the day following the fire we paid little attention to it. It was Sunday and a neighbor was visiting us at the time, and because she was just about to make her departure, we were standing in our lane near her car.

We had our backs to the camper, but Selena, our neighbor, faced it and both Frank and I wheeled in an about-face as she remarked: "Oh, look! Hawk's brought a friend home with him!"

Hawk limped toward us and the grin on his face was as wide as the world. The slight figure of what appeared to be a litle girl followed him, clinging to his hand and holding back. Hawk drew her toward us.

It was a girl, all right, of indeterminate age; barefoot; in a shapeless dress that appeared to be made out of flour sacks. She had hair the color of damp sand and it hung, straight and fine, to her waist, falling forward so that it hid her face.

Selena, Frank, and I stood in the blazing sun, speechless. Somewhere a rooster crowed and Gloria, the guinea, let out a few throaty buck-wheats.

Hawk and his hesitant companion faced us—also speechless.

The silence ballooned ominously.

Selena spoke first.

"Is this a friend of yours, Hawk?" she asked politely.

"This here's m'wife!" roared Hawk and he let out a guffaw that scattered chickens, cats, colts, and ground squirrels in a mile-wide radius around us.

I caught a glimpse of Frank's expression out of the tail of my eye and never had I seen such a look of incredulity on any man's face. After all, he had not been psychologically prepared for this contretemps, as I had.

Silence threatened to engulf us. It seemed to flow into the vacuum left by Hawk's laugh, as thunder rolls in after lightning.

Selena, who is the soul of graciousness, widely traveled and socially suave—a woman who manages to preserve the amenities even in our hinterland—seemed unable to utter another word.

I realized I had to say something.

As a word weaver I am seldom at a loss for words, but this time the loom was empty.

"Your wedding was rather unexpected, wasn't it, Hawk?" I managed at last.

"I been fixin' t' git hitched fer quite a spell," boomed Hawk. "This 'un here, jes' didn' know it!" He looked down at the drooping figure whose bowed head came no higher than his hip bone, and poked at her with a huge finger.

She remained silent, head bowed.

"What's your wife's name, Hawk?" I asked.

"Tell 'em yore name, Punk," Hawk roared.

A small voice emerged from the clouds of hair.

"Loraline."

"I hope you'll be very happy, Loraline," said Selena. Her voice was unexpectedly tender.

The head lifted, the hair fell back, and we beheld a child-like face of delicate beauty. It was devoid of make-up; the features neatly composed and regular; the eyes, the clear amber of hounds' eyes.

As she raised her head Loraline's glance met Hawk's and instantly she smiled and her whole being seemed to emit a glowing radiance.

Why this shy creature loved Hawk!

The discovery sent romantic shivers up my spine. Women are slobs in situations like this and I am no exception.

My ecstatic mood was shattered by the chill of Frank's voice:

"Just where do you expect to keep this—this—woman!" he demanded.

"Loraline and me'll do nicely in the cabin," Hawk replied calmly. He grinned toothlessly at the sweet small face lifted so trustingly to his and rested a huge paw on Loraline's shoulder, completely enveloping it.

"You'll make out there as long as it takes you to find another job!" snapped Frank and strode off.

"I really must be going," said Selena hastily, and she slipped into her little sports car. "Heaven help you," she whispered, for my ears alone, and peeled out the lane.

I waved to Selena and turned to look at the result of my incurable desire to match mates. Of all the sins that weigh on my conscience, surely this weighed the heaviest! Still I had never seen Hawk look so happy. As for Loraline, one couldn't tell. She certainly loved him, if I read the message that flashed in the clear amber eyes. But love is subject to so many interpretations . . .

"Mr. Griffith won't be quite as angry in the morning, Hawk," I said, with far more assurance than I felt.

"I know, ma'am!"

The lovers strolled toward the cabin and I turned to follow Frank. It would take some clever word handling to extricate myself from this one.

But then I thought of something I felt certain would bring a smile to Frank's lips. I tracked him to the den where he was puffing up a storm on his pipe.

"Say, honey, I bet this is the first time in history that cupid's little arrow ever brought down a hawk . . ."

"Wherever did Hawk find you, Loraline?" I asked his bare-foot bride next day as we hung out the wash together. She confessed that she had no other possessions except the shift in which she was married; not even a toothbrush. But she did own a pair of panties and a bra and these we had scrubbed and bleached till they almost looked clean.

I half expected Loraline to say that Hawk had found her beneath a fern frond or perhaps found her hiding under a conch shell, therefore I was totally unprepared for the calm statement: "I was tending bar in El Coyote."

Ask an inquisitive question and you get what you deserve for an answer.

"Hawk cain't hold his likker, it makes him ornery," she said without any rancor. "I told him I'd be a wife to him long as he laid off the stuff but not a minute longer," she added with surprising firmness.

"I suppose you know how to cook," I said, thinking of Hawk's insatiable appetite. (There never was any doubt in Frank's mind or mine that he had worn his teeth away eating, probably at a very early age.)

"Oh, yes'm," smiled Loraline and standing in her shift in the dappled sunlight, with her hair falling around her shoulders, she didn't look a day over fourteen.

"How old are you, Loraline?" I asked with a directness I hoped might prompt a true answer. When women ask questions, they don't usually stop till they satisfy their entire curiosity.

"Twenty-three, ma'am."

I almost fell over.

"Loraline. You're not."

"Yes'm. I am."

There was no use pursuing this conversation. Since moving to ranch country, I had discovered that lies come easy to certain segments of the populace.

"You sure had me fooled," I said. "I though you weren't old enough to be out of grade school."

She laughed her trilling little-girl laugh which caused Hawk to materialize from behind a towering pyrocantha bush. He grabbed her and swung her high over his head so that her shift which was halfway up her thigh, went considerably higher. I had a feeling I should retire to the kitchen and did.

In the two weeks that the honeymooners remained with us Loraline never left Hawk's side except when he thrust her into the kitchen and told her she had to help me with the cooking.

Hawk's intentions were good in doing this but how I wished that he would just let his little bride follow him about like a puppy and leave me to struggle with the chow making alone.

Loraline insisted on making angel cake one day because she said it was Hawk's favorite. She overlooked one small detail: She forgot to put in the flour. The result was a cake that came out of the oven about six inches tall but on cooling collapsed to the thickness of a wafer.

Loraline tried her hand at biscuits next and neglected to put in the baking powder.

Even the guineas had trouble coping with that culinary catastrophe.

But when Frank blustered, as he did hourly, "Hawk and

that girl have to go . . ." I would quickly say, "Now, honey
. . . Loraline helps me with the cooking." He had seen Loraline
in the kitchen, stirring and beating, so how could he know
that everything she made had been consumed either by Lady
or the cats or the chickens.

"We just can't turn them out, Frank. They don't have a cent
and not a thing in this world, not even a toothbrush . . ."

"Hawk doesn't need a toothbrush; he doesn't have any
teeth . . ."

He had me there but I continued rapidly: "Loraline has no
clothes, only that one dress to her name . . ."

"If you call that a dress . . it doesn't go below her navel . . ."

"We can't turn them out . . ."

"Do you mean we've got to support them for the rest of
our lives?"

This did sound pretty drastic.

"Well, not exactly . . ."

"I think I've got another job lined up for Hawk."

"Oh you angel!" I was so relieved I grabbed Frank and
kissed him.

"What's that for?"

"For being so good and kind and thoughtful and getting
Hawk a job so they can leave here . . ."

"I thought you couldn't bear to part with them because
she's so much help with the cooking." When I said nothing,
he added: "Or are you afraid the cats and the chickens will
starve without her little goodies?"

"Must you always know everything!" I cried, now really
furious. "When can he start the new job, what is it, where
is it?"

"Well if you're not a fraud. Pretending you were so happy
to have a bride and groom on the premises and now you
can't wait to get them out of here. The job is caretaker over
at the Carter place and they get living quarters and Hawk
can do some odd jobs on the side and they ought to make

enough to live on if he doesn't start swacking the bottle again."
"Let's tell them right away and help them pack."

We piled odds and ends of furniture in the Camino to set
Hawk and his bride up in hosekeeping and I sneaked enough
clothing out of trunks and closets to outfit Loraline for several
months. I even threw in a few romantic extras like cologne
and hair spray and dusting powder and eye shadow . . . a
bride needs some kind of booster after the first stage of her
honeymoon if she wants to keep rocketing.

Hawk and Loraline were delighted with their new home.
Hawk was really proud of his job and it was much easier for
him than ranch work, which made Frank feel good because he
thought Hawk attempted too much with his bad hip.

When I cleaned out the cabin this time I found enough
cigarette butts to fill a bucket (but no sign of hard liquor.)
There were also hundreds of crumpled and coverless comic
books, and a gigantic assortment of very dirty and very holey
socks. (Apparently Hawk had never washed any all the time
he'd been with us.)

Poor shabby cabin, who will call you home next time, I
wondered.

What dreams and hopes, what fears or tears will you share?
What a story your four walls could tell of lonely lives and lonely
people . . .

I swept the last of the dirt out the back door and placed the
cabin key under the kerosene can on the back stoop where
the next occupant could find it.

Hawk and Loraline hadn't gone very far away. Would we
ever see either of them again?

As it turned out, we did, because Loraline gave a housewarming and we were invited. We arrived bearing a student
lamp and a colorful bedspread as our housewarming gifts.

The little house was clean; the furniture representative of
early Spanish, 1929 modern and scatterings of Mission Oak;

the whole was enlivened by Hawk and Loraline touches, including massive deer horns, dusty paper floral bouquets, and long legged dolls in satin pajamas. (I hadn't seen any since my John Held days and decided they must have been contributed by one of Loraline's relatives.)

We sat tensely on a sofa which had one caster missing and an arm glued in place and drank warm Coca Cola and ate a really luscious chocolate cake. How had Loraline managed to accomplish it? I complimented her on the cake without daring to ask how she happened to get in all the required ingredients.

"That gal sure can make chocolate cake," Frank whispered to me. It happens to be his favorite.

As we were leaving, we walked through the kitchen, and there, on the table, I noticed another chocolate cake with a deep depression in the center.

Loraline's eye met mine as I hastily looked away from it and she slipped over to whisper in my ear.

"That's my cake," she giggled. "I forgot the flour. Hawk bought the cake you ate from the bread truck."

I noticed several loaves of bread stacked near the dejected cake and nearby on the drainboard there were three or four giant size cans of tuna.

"You have married a man of king-size appetites, Loraline," I thought to myself as I watched her patter on her bare feet toward Hawk who had entered the kitchen. "Let us hope you can satisfy them."

Her hair fell about her shoulders and she smiled shyly up at her gargantuan husband. He swung her high above him with a pink-gummed grin.

"I've got nothing to worry about," I decided, as Frank and I pulled away from the tiny house in the Camino. "Loraline may be no bigger than a sparrow but she's one sparrow that tamed a Hawk."

16

Philo, a Mighty Sharp Character

The state emplyoment office was declared "out of bounds" and Frank cancelled our subscription to the L.A. *Times* and we settled down to another halcyon period of help-lessness.

In no time I became a professional pooper scooper and could muck a stall and sling manure as expertly as any stable-man.

I watched the corrals with practiced eye and as soon as its four-footed occupant sullied it I was on the spot with wheelbarrow and shovel, tidying things up.

"What are you trying to do, keep the corrals as clean as your kitchen?" cried Frank.

"Some of my friends wouldn't consider that too difficult," I retorted.

"After you haul the ashes out of the wood stove the kitchen could stand a good shoveling."

I followed up my stall muckings with generous sprinklings of lime, cleaned out the watering troughs regularly, kept the feed measured and ready to go for the next feeding and made sure everything was squared away and locked up before retiring. The ranch had never looked so neat; the animals had never been so pampered; and at seven o'clock every night, when I finally sat down for the first time during the day, I would fall asleep two minutes after turning on the seven o'clock news and remain lifeless as a log until summoned to duty at six A.M. the following morning.

"Well, do you want me to hire a hand?" Frank asked, after three weeks of this. It was I who made the ultimatum this time: "No help for us!"

Too proud to acknowledge that every bone and every muscle groaned in protest, too stubborn to reveal the fact that my hands were covered with callouses, I hedged a bit. "Maybe if we got a nice single hand from an employment agency—" I didn't mention the State man. I was ashamed to ask him for any further assistance. They really must have thought we were orges, considering the constant turnover of help that we had.

"Okay. You pick the employment agency," said Frank magnanimously.

I flew to the Yellow Pages and let my fingers do the selecting for me, just the way they show in the advertisements.

That night I stayed up to watch the Late Show. I could afford to live civilized. The Acme Employment Agency informed us that they had a "reliable ranch hand" scheduled to arrive first thing in the morning. "You'll be able to turn him loose on the chores without worry or reservation because this fellow's a farm boy and used to hard work."

The mere thought of not having to shovel manure at daybreak set me to thinking I was a lady. I washed all the hay chaff and horse dander out of my hair and set it a new way. I put on fingernail polish and luxuriated in a hot both. The following morning I put on a clean white shirt and spotless tan breeches. I even polished my boots and rubbed some hand lotion over my callouses.

Then I sat down to a second cup of coffee while we waited for our new hand to arrive.

The man from the Acme Employment Agency rolled in with him at one o'clock in a shiny new station wagon.

By then I had mucked five stalls; cleaned out six corrals; curried four horses and scrubbed out eight watering tubs. My shirt was stained with sweat; my breeches were streaked with horse slobber; my boots were hoary with wet straw and manure clusters. My hair was hanging in shreds and half of my nail polish was chipped off my nails.

I was just plodding toward the house to rustle up a belated lunch when the Acme Wagon ground to a halt and two figures emerged from it.

"Got a little lost and drove about a hundred miles out of our way," said the Acme man, extending a hand to Frank. "But we didn't lose your new hand."

"Philo Budge," said the little fellow who followed him.

He wrung Frank's hand like a plump handle, then proffered an employment ID card..

We couldn't believe it!

He wore overalls! The Big Hank kind with shoulder straps and flapping legs. We hadn't seen anything like them since we left the East.

He also wore G.I. boots and an upturned straw hat set atop a shock of flaming red hair. He was short, slight, but wiry and greatly resembled in appearance the well-known comedy star, Sterling Holloway, only he was much smaller.

"Don't forget, Philo, you owe us a week's pay, payable within thirty days," said the gentleman from Acme, towering over Philo. "Here's a stamped, addressed envelope for your convenience in mailing it. Be glad to supply any additional ranch help you may require, Mr. Griffith," he added affably. "We specialize in strictly reliable help, thoroughly investigated, with excellent references and ample experience. Here's my card. Call any time. We're open Sunday. Well, I'd best be getting along. Good luck to you, Philo."

The Acme representative was still talking as the shiny new station wagon purred out of sight.

Philo was all ours.

"Show Philo to his cabin, I've got a horse tied I've got to see to," said Frank and promptly disappeared.

"Come this way, Philo."

He picked up his plastic suitcase.

"Nice place you got here," he said with difficulty. It was obvious that he was pitifully ill at ease and making conversation cost him considerable effort.

"I hope you like it," I said. "Do you know how to cook for yourself?"

"No'm. I can't cook worth a hog waller."

"Well, you can take your meals with us then," I said. I'd probably regret this surge of magnanimity but the die was cast and Philo didn't look as if he could hold too much food; certainly nothing like Hawk's capacity.

"I don't hear too good so I hope it don't bother you none if I talk kinda loud," said Philo. I'd noticed he was shouting but had attributed it to nervousness.

"It won't bother us," I said, automatically raising my voice a notch.

"Got an ear drum popped out in the war," he explained.

He had eyes like bits of bright blue glass and the most engaging, mischievous smile. He didn't seem a day over twenty. "You look too young to have been in the war, Philo."

"I was in the Korean War. Enlisted when I was sixteen and they didn't find out I'd falsified the records till it was too late and I was over there. I was parachute jumpin' on my sixteenth birthday. Ain't as young as I look neither. I'm thirty-two."

I was astonished.

"Well you are fooling the public!"

He laughed at this and for the first time some of the tenseness dissolved and he took off the straw hat and wiped his narrow, freckled face with a red bandana handkerchief.

"Why I ain't got no cause to be skeered o' you or this place," he said, marvelling "Yore jest plain, ordinary folks. Yessir," he repeated, drawling out the words as if they were a revelation to him. "Yore just plain, ordinary folks."

It was the first time I'd been called ordinary right to my face but the way Philo said it he made it sound good.

"There's just no folks more ordinary than us, Philo," I said. "When you've been with us a while you'll find it out."

Philo was not afraid of work; he embraced it. The harder it was the more he enjoyed it. If there was a difficult and strenuous way of tackling any chore, that was the way he tackled it.

Philo also like to talk. And the subject he liked most to talk about was Tennessee, his home state.

"Back home," Philo would shout, "we wouldn't countenance these here horses standin' around eatin' their weight in feed. No'm'm. M' dad'd put 'em t' work. M' real dad, that is, not m' step dad. M' real dad wouldn't have nothing to do with us kids. He finally died, fer a mercy, and m' maw married m' step dad and m' step dad y' might say raised us, me 'n m' two brothers . . . ."

I was making corn bread and trying to remember whether I'd put in two cups of corn meal or one and whether the baking powder was in yet, and while I was listening to Philo's commentary, the corn bread was getting the worst of the deal.

"Dad, m' real dad, not m' step dad, didn't keer much fer animals," said Philo. "That's how come he was flung outta church. Dad caught a sow stealin' feed from the chickens so he put her eyes out so she couldn't see to do it no more . . . "

I dropped the measuring cup in the batter.

"Your dad did what!"

"M' real dad," said Philo. His blue eyes blazed like live

coals. "It's the God's honest truth, ma'am. Dad, m' real dad, put the sow's eyes out and the church folk seed this blind sow on our place and found out Dad done it so they flung him clear outta the church. Didn't bother dad none. He never went to church anyway."

I looked at Philo with such horror he backed off uneasily.

"Dad, m' real dad, he was a rough man," he said, by way of explanation. That's why I was so glad when maw married m' step dad. Only by then I was hot fer fightin' so I joined the Army and anyway both m' brothers was in jail. One on the count o' rape and t'other fer robbin' a post office . . . "

I gave up trying to make cornbread and turned on Philo in anger.

"Philo, if you're making up these things you can stop right now," I cried, waving a wooden spoon at him. "I'm not impressed and I don't like listening to fibs."

"I ain't a-makin' 'em up," shouted Philo, not giving an inch. "They're all true, you kin look it the record. It warn't real rape the girl was jes lyin' about her age. And the brother robbed the post office he weren't aimin' to steal nohtin'; jes did it fer a prank. Only got nine dollars. But they got him in jail 'cause it were a federal offence and he's servin' ten years." He howled with laughter. "Joke was on him all right. Got less'n a dollar a year."

With this he thwomped out of the kitchen, overalls flapping and his straw hat riding the waves of flame-red hair, G.I. boots shaking the floor boards.

I was so undone I knew I shouldn't try to finish the cornbread for lunch since it has a way of reflecting my emotional vibrations and it would be bound to have a lump in the middle.

After lunch I got Frank aside.

"How do you feel about Philo!" I began, tentatively.

"He's okay. Kooky but okay. He works twice as hard as three mules and with about as much planning, but he does more work here in a day than those other clods did in a month. I like him."

"He comes from a mighty strange family. His father was a monster and he has two brothers in jail and he was in the army when he was only sixteen . . . "

"In the Army—are you kidding!"

"In Korea. And besides, he isn't as young as you thought he was. He's thirty-two!"

"Thirty-two! That little pipsqueak!"

"He may be little but he's strong as an ox. I saw him lift the ranch truck out of a rut the other day all by himself."

"That's what I mean. The tougher the job the better he likes it. Don't you start messing around now. I've finally got somebody here not afraid of work. You just keep out of things."

I know when I have my come upance. I kept my mouth shut. For at least a day.

Then Philo cornered me when I was rinsing out clothes and hanging them out by the woodshed.

"Back home maw don't fool around with this way o' doin' clothes any more," said Philo. (I kept count one time and decided ninety-nine out of every hundred utterances made by Philo led off with the words: "back home.") "I got her one of them electric home laundries. She just dumps the clothes in the washer and then flings 'em in the dryer and she don't have any of this hangin' out to do."

It seemed pointless to explain to Philo that the reason we couldn't have any modern home laundry equipment was because the ranch water was half iron and half limestone and it ate up pipes and plumbing and washer mechanisms faster than Jonathan could gobble up corn.

"Here, let me help," and Philo grabbed an armful of dripping clothes, shoved a fluting of clothes pegs in his mouth and began lining up blue jeans and work shirts against the blaring blue backdrop of sky.

It wasn't for several seconds, when I turned to hand him a bulky sheet and he happened to have his back turned toward me, that I noticed the knife. It was a long hunting knife and it hung in a leather sheath, in the middle of Philo's back, hitched to the belt of his jeans.

Philo turned as my eyes were still glued to it and my expression must have caught his attention for he stopped.

"What's the matter?" he cried. "You see a snake or somethin'?"

"N . . . it's n . . nothing," I stammered, "hurry up with those clothes so I can go in and get lunch started."

I practically ran to Frank as soon as I could get my hands dried.

"Philo's carrying a great big knife in the backof his jeans!" I cried.

"I know. He likes it there where he can reach it in a hurry if he wants to cut loose a horse or defend himself against Indians," Frank laughed.

"You knew it was there all the time?"

"I've noticed it the last couple of days or so."

"And it doesn't seem odd to you?"

"No odder than a lot of things that go on around here," Frank twinkled, seeing that I was really in a state and imagining he could tease me out of it.

"Well it sure seems strange to me. And scary, too."

"Don't you worry about it. Philo's kooky. He admits it . . ."

"Admits it!"

"Says he comes from a whole family of kooks. But he's a good worker. Now leave him alone. I've got my eye on him. He likes knives. And he likes to keep them sharp . . . "

"Good heavens!"

"Well what good's a knife if it doesn't have an edge on it?"

"Oh you're giving me the bizz and I hate you!" I ran for the house.

I was ironing, the chore I hate most, the next time Philo came by for a little chit chat.

"How come you don't have a big vicious dog around here?" he asked.

"Why in heaven's name would we?"

"To keep thieves and meddlers away."

"We're not troubled by thieves and meddlers."

"Back home we allus kept a dog would chew anybody up what set foot on the place. All the neighbors did, too. Once't a neighbor's dog got loose and came over and killed some of our chickens. Dad . . m' real dad . . not m' step dad . . he went right over to the neighbor's and shot it."

"Shot a neighbor's dog on his own land without any warning or not even proof the neighbor's dog was at fault?"

"Dad had proof all right. He saw blood on the dog and he knowed it was blood from our chickens."

"Now really . . how could anyone know . . "

"Who was gonna argue after the dog was dead?"

Philo squatted down near the ironing board, pulled a whetstone out of his jean's pocket, slipped the knife out of its scabbard on the back of his belt and began sharpening it slowly and patiently as he talked. After several strokes on the whetstone he would hold it to the light, run his thumb over it and return to sharpening it sedulously.

I said nothing. But I ironed several wrinkles in Frank's good town shirt, trying to keep one eye on the knife.

"It ain't easy to kill your first man," said Philo unexpectedly. "But after the first one it ain't hard at all."

"Philo. Really. What makes you say things like that . . . "

"Thinkin' about Korea. I often think of it. I was just a baby really. The guy came at me. And I knifed him. The knife was all bloody. I got sick. But I didn't get sick the next time. I laughed instead. 'Cause it was so easy."

"Don't you think you should try to forget that, Philo?" I asked him gently. I could suddenly see and, more important, feel, what had happened to this boy. Accustomed as he was "back home" to cruelty, he had been flung into the middle of war when he was still much too young to be able to cope with it.

He looked up at me, the freckled face drawn and looking old suddenly.

"I've tried," he said. "It won't leave me. It won't leave me be."

"Maybe if you got out more with young people . . . found a nice girl."

"Oh girls won't have nothin' to do with me, say I'm too rough," said Philo with candor. "I wanted to marry one oncet, back home. I got a trailer house with my veteran's benefits, set it in the middle of a corn field. It was so purty." His face now was youthful and tender. "I put everything in it fer her. Copper bottom pots and pans and a TV set and ruffly curtains. She come to look at it and I grabbed her and kissed her like I was never gonna let go. She run off and never come back. No, girls won't have nothin' to do with me," he repeated. And honed his knife.

"Philo, weren't you ever told that you're supposed to trust your neighbor and be friends with him?" I asked.

I was mending an accumulation of buttonless work shirts, holey socks and rent jackets. The temperature had dropped to thirty, which is equal to ten where houses are sieves and the only heat supply is a wood stove and fireplace. And it seemed a good time for indoor chores. Philo sat cross-legged at my feet and not just his trusty hunting knife but a whole array of knives of various shapes and sizes lay stretched out before him. I had grown accustomed to the fact that it did something for Philo to be able to hone his knives; slowly, meticulously. And he liked our talks together.

"No'm. That wasn't the way I was brung up," he said with his customary forthrightness. "We was told shoot yer neighbor, afore he shoots you, and many a time we had a close call gettin' the fust shot fired."

"But Philo, that's unhealthy. It makes people sick inside to hate. I grant you a lot of people seem mighty unlovable. But we're supposed to try to love them. That's what the Bible tells us to do."

"I reckon you ain't never had to cut up a man so's not to give him time to cut you up," said Philo.

"No," I said thoughtfully. "I've never had to defend my life, as you have, in war, by taking another life. I suppose if it came right down to it, I could. But you think about that so much and there are so many other things you could think about . . . I mean besides knives and war . . ."

"Knives come in handy. I like to know they're ready to do whatever's expected of them." He chuckled and set the whetstone aside and looked up at me, his eyes so blue it hurt.

"I could wisht I'd a knowed a family like you when I was younger," he said. "I've watched you since I've been here. You and the Mister allus so kindly intentioned to one another. And don't never lock nothin' up, don't even have a gun at your bedside. Trustin' people fer feed and horses . . . Sure ponders me to think on it."

"Maybe we're fortunate, but nobody has ever tried to cheat us . . . or harm us," I said. "We've always believed what you look for in others you usually get."

Philo smiled, one of his rare smiles, the puckish smile of a freckle-faced red-headed boy.

"Sure ponders me," he said, and reached for his whetstone.

The next day Philo asked permission to take the ranch truck up to the woods for something he had to tend to.

"Do you have a license to drive?" asked Frank. "Not that you need it driving on the ranch here, but I just wondered in case you wanted to go in town on your own some time."

"I don't have no license," snapped Philo, drawing his brows together, and he jumped in the ranch truck and slammed the door.

"He sure is getting kookier by the minute," said Frank as the truck disappeared through the trees. "Maybe you're right and we ought to ask him to move on."

"Why I never said any such thing," I cried hotly. "Philo's just a poor kid who's never known anything but cruelty and it's good for him being here. Did you notice how he's relaxed lately? He even whistles once in a while."

"He still works like he was mowing his way through a platoon of guerrillas," said Frank. "I thought you were afraid of his emotional attachment for knives. He's got a whole arsenal of them now, I saw them in the cabin."

"The knives make him feel safe. No. I'm not afraid of Philo since I'm beginning to understand him. I think he needs something that maybe we can give him. Let's keep him here and find out."

Frank put an arm around me.

"You're not such a bad old woman," he said. "Just half bad."

So he was as fond of Philo as I was.

"You're all bad but I like you that way. Move along before I run this needle through you."

Philo returned with the ranch truck loaded with firewood. He had sawed up a whole tree and reduced the branches to kindling and he stacked it all neatly in the woodshed. Enough wood to last us two months of winter.

"No one on earth could saw that much wood in that time," said Frank when he saw the entire wood pile replenished.

"No one but me when I put m' mind to it," laughed Philo. He was dirty and sweaty but we had never seen him so happy. It was as if the physical effort of sawing wood had released all the pent-up tensions that had been bugging him and he could laugh and joke without the touchiness that always became apparent whenever we made any attempt at humor.

"I'll make you a chocolate cake for supper," I told him. And I did. I even wrote his name on it and trailed a silly saw after it with frosting.

"I sure like you folks," said Philo when he stuffed down the third helping. "I'll cut some more wood for you tomorrow."

"No need to cut any more wood, we've got enough for now . . . " said Frank.

The phone rang, interrupting him. I answered it. It was for Philo. The first call that had ever come for him since he'd been with us.

"Who's calling?" I asked.

"Beverly Grant at the Acme Employment Agency. I've got to talk to him right away!" The sense of urgency in the man's voice startled me. "Had he found another job for Philo? That would be a great trick to play on us!

Philo returned to the kitchen, after a very brief conversation, silent and pale.

"I'm hitting' the sack," he said curtly. "Thanks for everything," he added clumsily.

"Is anything wrong, Philo?" I asked.

"No'm." And he stalked out the door to his cabin.

The next day the man from the Acme Employment Agency drew up in his shiny new station wagon.

Philo was in the back pasture watering stock.

"Did you want to see Philo?" I asked him.

"No, I'd like to see your husband, Mrs. Griffith."

Frank appeared just then and I moved toward the house, feeling this was meant to be man-to-man talk.

I busied myself, tidying up, sensing something was very wrong; still I knew I had no right to meddle.

From the kitchen window I saw Philo return, join the two men, then go into his cabin. He came out with his plastic suitcase; his straw hat set back on his head. The sunlight fired his red hair to flame as it had the first day he came to us.

I knew that Philo was leaving and I felt a twist in my heart.

With our own boy in the Navy, Philo had become very much like a son. Whatever he was others had made him, including his parents. Whatever lay ahead for him now, I wished it might hold the promise of good.

When Frank came in his look told me instantly that whatever the Acme man had told him must have shocked him deeply.

"Philo escaped from the State Mental Hospital. He has a war neurosis. He falsified his records; that's how the Acme man happened to send him here. He was horrified when he discovered what he'd done. Philo is definitely not to be trusted around knives."

"Oh poor Philo! What will they do with him! I didn't even say goodbye!" The words met a boulder in my throat.

"Philo told me goodbye for you. They're taking him back to the hospital to continue his psychiatric treatment. They hope he still may pull out of it . . . "

I put off going to the cabin as long as I could.

It was clean and as undisturbed as if no one had ever lived in it.

The windows were open to the sweet air and sunshine; the bed was neatly made. The only evidence of Philo's occupancy was a row of sixteen knives of various shapes and sizes, lined up in a glittering array on top of the bureau.

I viewed them through splinters of tears.

Poor Philo! Whose was the sin, that made you become a soldier before you became a man?

17

Other Friends, Animal, Vegetable
and Questionable

"Don't you find ranch life very lonely after living for so many years in the city?" visitors to the Bar None frequently ask me.

"My answer is: "How could I possibly be lonely, surrounded by friends?"

I not only enjoy my long established friendships with the mares, the colts, the cats, and the chickens, there are countless other creatures who enrich our lives merely by sharing the ranch with us. Observant, cautious, and proud of their freedom, they have no desire to trade their independence for the dubious comforts of domesticity.

Among such friends I count the red-tailed hawk that soars above the Bar None meadows, plummeting to earth in a silent dive that ends in a juicy mouse dinner. The hoot owl that lives in the towering white oak remained for years no more than a pulsating throb in the night. Then we found him unconscious in the ranch lane. He had been struck by a car. Examination showed only slight wing damage. We kept him in the barn where he could feed on the rodents that pillage our grain and in three weeks he was healed and flew away. Now when we hear his rhythmic "Who? Who? we know who our nocturnal inquirer is, a handsome magnificently plumaged fellow whose clear amber eyes and haunty mien give him an air of remarkable superiority.

Quail, of course, are everywhere, attracted by the grain we broadcast for the horses. They scurry before us through the brush, the little forward-tilted topknots of the males dangling ahead of them like miner's lamps.

And when a saucy blue jay flirts his tail as he balances on our television antenna it reminds us that the bluebird of happiness is indeed to be found in our ranch yard and not beyond the encircling mountains.

The first time the red-winged blackbirds appeared at the ranch I was entranced by the beauty of their darkly gleaming feathers, delighted with the splash of their trilling liquid melodies. Then the little darlings took over. Thousands filled the live oaks, weaving a scarlet tapestry against the dark green leaves.

Endless their descending three-note cadences beat upon us till we seemed to drown in a sea of silver sound. The sweetness soon lost its savor and swelled to a compelling stridency. The temptation was great to evict the chattering songsters. But we have never knowingly been inhospitable to any wild creature seeking refuge at the ranch. At the end of a month, however, I was beginning to wonder just how many blackbirds could be baked in a pie. Then inexplicably, as suddenly as they arrived, the blackbirds left, never to reappear.

The quiet following their departure was thick as cotton.

For the first time we could communicate with one another without shouting.

As the mother of an energetic and inquisitive son I learned fairly early in life to tolerate snakes.

When our son was about twelve he managed a snake booth

at the Scoutcraft Fair and trained his exhibition at home. He would sit watching television while a beautiful king snake wound its way slowly up one arm, across his shoulders, and down the other arm.

Not content to become a snake expert himself, he soon instructed me in the ways of reptiles and I finally reached a point where I could handle his pet snakes and allow them to coil around my wrist while I patted them.

I found that a snake feels cool and dry to the touch. He is strong and supple in his movements; clean in his habits; certainly an animal that might be considered a friend; but I would rather he remain an acquaintance.

I was glad that I finally arrived at this comradely understanding of snakes, because one day I opened my kitchen cabinet and there, resting in my roasting pan, lay a husky, good-sized snake. I recognized it instantly as a gopher snake and therefore harmless, so without batting an eyelash, I got my kitchen nippers and gently lifted him by the neck and carried him outside where I turned him loose behind the wood pile.

What would my cell mates at the Squirrel Cage have thought of me? I wondered. But privately I was rather proud of my feat. I felt I had passed some sort of landmark in my transition from word slinger to ranch wife.

Rodents of every sort take up residence at the Bar None.
Not all of them exhibit company manners.

The gophers make a sieve of the back yard, and ounce for ounce of body weight they can remove more soil in less time than it would take a bulldozer to do the same job.

"Why don't you shoot the worthless critters?" the ranch hands want to know.

"I'd like to some time when they nibble at the roots of my flowers and cut off the saplings as fast as we plant them. But actually their tunnels make the soil porous and receptive to rain so they lessen flood damage."

This is too much for the hands. They usually turn away, shaking their heads sadly.

But it's a fact that rain water runs through the gopher channels deep into the earth where it can more readily arrive at the water table feeding our well.

The ground squirrels are as ubiquitous as the gophers. They occupy a bank of cliff dwellings along one side of the lower pasture that resembles a prehistoric Indian pueblo. Although all the openings appear to be exactly alike, each ground squirrel manages to slip into his particular burrow at the first hint of danger, faster than an eye wink. I've never seen one enter a neighbor's house by mistake, which is more than you can say for many tract dwellers.

The ground squirrels are fey, prankish, mischievous. They will wait till the guineas stroll past their village, then leap out of their burrows and scare the wits out of them. When this happens Gloria heads for the woods with a scream of terror and Granville leaps straight into the air and they both emit bloodcurdling squawks.

In the barn we have the rats. I can find nothing admirable about rats though I'm sure they must have their purpose in the web of life. Fortunately the cats—not Slinky and his kitty-cat pack, but the wild litters raised in the brush—know how to cope with these marauders.

Indoor we have the mice. The ranch house is ancient, far from water proof, cold proof, or mouse proof; so the mice have their way with us.

Sometimes in the middle of the night I can hear one run his teeth across the moulding like a naughty boy dragging chalk across the blackboard.

Once I started to make the bed and a mouse jumped out from between the blankets. At another time I picked up a dish towel and a mouse flew out of it, hurtled through the air, and landed in the corn bread batter. Experiences of this sort can prove rather shattering.

Frank always laughed at my mouse jitters. Then one morning he turned on the stove griddle and a mouse jumped out of the grease bin. It ran the entire length of the red hot griddle before it dropped to the floor and disappeared. For years after the incident we would recognize the precocious visitor. His feet were burned on the griddle as a result of this experience and we could spot him because from then on he walked with a limp.

The lizards make themselves as much at home as the mice. We have many varieties, from the tiny, sere, chameleon-types that resemble dried leaves and move with the speed of light; to huge rat-tail lizards boasting tails a foot long. One time I reached in the closet for a sweater, felt something move beneath my fingers, and pulled my hand back to find part of Mr. Lizard's elegant tail in my grasp.

My son quickly quieted my fears.

"Don't worry, mother," he said. "A lizard always re-grows its tail."

I expect to find animals in the bureau drawers, behind the shower curtain, living happily in the Christmas Tree ornaments and nestled in my snuggies. But I still come unglued when I meet up with wasps.

Over the years wasps have managed to build snug, secret houses in the attic and there they live quietly most of the year, attending to their own duties, raising their families, and leaving us strictly alone. For this I am grateful. I know there must be something lovable about a wasp but I fail to discern it.

Whenever the weather gets really hot and the attic becomes an inferno, the entire wasp population descends to the comparative coolness of our bedroom.

At such times there is a great flopping and flailing about; Frank cusses and curses bugs in general and wasps in particular. He vows he'll get rid of the so and sos forever. But he never can figure out how.

Then I made the most amazing discovery.

If we leave the air conditioner on day and night, it cools the attic and the wasps stay in their hideaway and out of our bedroom. Now as soon as the temperature goes above ninety, I run for the air conditioner. Let it run, say I. It's a lot easier to use than Raid, costs less than the exterminator—and it really isn't a bit of fun to roll over in bed one night and find yourself impaled on a wasp's javelin.

Bobcats, mountain lions, coyotes, and other less civilized quadrupeds make regular visits to the Bar None but they have never molested us. When the colts are young Frank keeps a gun handy in case an intruder should overstep the bounds of friendliness. But I am thankful to say that we have never had any reason to be ungracious to any of our visitors to date.

One summer when our son was young we entertained a troop of Boy Scouts at the ranch and they slept in their sleeping bags under the stars.

The phone rang in the middle of the night and Frank picked it up, mistaking the ring for our party line ring, since he was still half asleep.

He overheard the sheriff telling a deputy that a mountain lion was loose in the hills and a posse was being formed to track him down.

A group of sleepy, wondering Boy Scouts were hustled indoors, post haste, and Frank kept in touch with hte sheriff's office throughout the remainder of the night.

At dawn the lion was found crouching beneath a picnic table at a nearby roadside rest. He was not a mountain lion but a movie lion that had escaped from an animal trainer's ranch in the hills. He had appeared many times on television and his trainer confessed that he hadn't a tooth in his head.

I would love very much to number flowers among my ranch friends. But the gophers devour them at one end while the chickens gobble them up at the other; and so few are the flowers I've been able to raise.

I've tried geraniums, canna, hollyhocks, and oleander—plants which will grow unattended almost any place in Southern California.

But they won't grow for me—at least not in any normal fashion.

My hollyhocks develop stalks as big around as boa constrictors, shoot up higher than Jack's famous beanstalk, and then threaten me with leaves the size of elephant ears. However, they never produce any flowers.

A native Californian explained why. She said it was because I watered them too shallowly and too frequently. Seems you're supposed to water them about once every ten days and let the water sink down several feet. I haven't the patience for this proper method of plant watering; I prefer to sprinkle every evening. (Sprinkling is a lot lighter than other chores I could be doing at that particular time.) But sprinkling results in floral monstrosities.

I was about ready to give up flowers altogether when I discovered that cactus will thrive on our iron-clad, unfriendly soil. With virtually no encouragement my prickly pear cactus spread till it formed huge, hedge-like masses along the fences, at either end of the stables—it almost engulfed the pump house —and I never had to water it. I was right proud of it.

Then one day a couple drove into the ranch in a gleaming black Continental bearing Texas license plates. They eased themselves out of the car and they were both tall and handsome as Texans should be. They wore white Stetsons, white cowboy boots, white jeans tighter than their hide, flashing silver belt buckles, and bolo ties—but it was their his-and-her shirts that held our attention. They were white satin with a scattering of black polka dots across the back.

They introduced themselves as Quince and Holly Bronson, Appaloosa Breeders, and the significance of the polka dots became clear to us—the shirts were spotted in the manner of an Appaloosa's rump.

They heard we raised Appaloosas and had dropped by to see our spring crop.

As Frank explained that we had stopped breeding Appaloosas because we didn't get enough spotted colts, I looked at Holly. She was lean and long-limbed, had a beautiful and perfectly made up face; her hair, which was a rich mahogany brown, hung to her hips in two curling ringlets.

I was about to ask her to come inside for a cup of coffee when she suddenly spied the rolling sea of cactus that stretched away on every side. Her carefully outlined, heavily mascaraed eyes flew open and she pointed a white gloved hand in the direction of the spiny outgrowth.

"Is that there honest-to-Gawd cactus?" she cied in a drawl rich as butter.

"That's what it is!" I snapped. I was beginning to feel mighty mean, which is the way I usually feel when gorgeous babes drop by in streamlined breeches and slide a glance down their nose at me. Especially when I'm padding around in granny boots and pooper scooping slop slacks.

"Let's get out of heah, Quincy, honey," Holly called to her beautiful husband, and scooped her arm through his. "Back home," she said, "the only thing that hangs out with cactus is rats!"

Her comment unleashed a very spate of meanness. It rose up in me like a flood and I was framing a really sizzling retort when I noticed that Egbert, our maverick rooster, was sneaking up on Holly from the rear. He moved with the goose-stepping sideways motion that indicates he is getting ready for a flash flank attack.

I could have issued a warning.

But I didn't.

Egbert let Holly have it with both spurs and his rapier beak, right in the seat of her shiny white pants.

Holly let out a screech followed by some pure Anglo Saxon and leaped several feet in the air. She landed in a batch of slippery horse doo which slid out from under her, and, reaching for air, down she went in the goop, right smack on her shiny white bottom.

It doesn't sound like a good beginning for a friendship, but by the time Quince and Holly left the Bar None, several hours later, we had actually become good friends.

We invited them into the house so that Holly could change into a fresh pair of glittering white pants (she had dozens of them) and over several cups of coffee we learned that Holly and Quince were Roman riders in a traveling rodeo and raised Appaloosas on the side.

And whether they had access to heap good medicine or were just lucky, they'd had a lot more spotted colts than we had; almost ninety per cent!

Holly apologized for being sticky about the cactus and I apologized for not telling her, in time, that Egbert was a fink. Frank and Quince exchanged horse yarns—each trying to tell the biggest lie, the way horesemen aways do—then we looked at pictures of Quince and Holly's ranch in Texas, their prize-winning Appys, and publicity stills of their rodeo act.

When they left they promised to drop by next time they were up our way. That year, at Christmas, Holly sent me a handsome collection of baby cacti. It included over a hundred distinct varieties. I planted them on the Indian like mound of dirt that encases our cesspool and they grew and grew and multiplied and had pups (the name for cactus babies) and all summer long they produce the most fantastic Disney-like flowers. People come from miles around to see them and they all say I must have ten green thumbs to produce such gorgeous blooms. But Frank won't let me take the credit. He's sure the cesspool has something to do with it.

Some say diamonds are a girl's best friend. Among my best

friends I number mountains. The mountains that circle the Bar None are constant, watchful companions. In their stern and forbidding moods the mountains tower above us like threatening, brown-shouldered giants. But more often they sprawl like fecund Goddesses, their swollen bellies raised to the sky. The mountains remind us that there is solidity and substance to life.

When the mountains accept you as a friend they give you freely of their treasures: heady scent of sage; scarlet impact of wild fuchsia; pale mist of maiden's breath; and the heart-shaking beauty of rocks.

Until you've discovered the infinite variety and wonder of rock formations you haven't really savored the riches of a mountain friendship.

The way it happened to me . . .

I was slipping, sliding, crawling, climbing up the face of a Bar None mountain, and at the crest I came upon a rock clear and smooth as pale marble that resembled sea spume captured in stop motion.

How could anything so ceamy-white, cool, and translucent come out of this scarred, punished earth?

That was the rock that hooked me.

From that day I became the most avid rock hound. And now I have a truly fabulous collection of diamond-bright quartz crystal; polished jasper; mottled agate—all native to our region. I must confess that a neighboring ranch friend who is a really expert rock hunter contributed most of them. But I've learned to find a good share of my own.

Scrabbling through gorges and sliding down washes and tramping over old stream beds I've found not only exquisite rock specimens but the jaw bones of animals, Indian arrowheads, petrified wood and shells—the treasures yielded up by the mountains are inexhaustible.

I take a rasp and an old bucket, put on boots and a cap and away I go. Here is a hobby that requires no outlay of cash that drains away every care and worry and leaves your soul shining clean. It's the most fun to hunt rock specimens during the rainy season when the streams are running and nature deposits her bounty right in your lap!

What cataclysmic experience, what endless cycles of time, of heat, and of pressure combine to produce these stones of dazzling brilliance! This is the mystery and the wonder that keeps the rock hound on the trail. You can't explain it to anyone except a fellow rock hound. But once rock hunting gets you by the tail there's no escaping it.

Rock hunting is a glorious outlet that I rceommend to anyone who wants to work off pounds; drop off cares, and discover a whole new world of hidden beauty beneath their feet.

In spite of Frank's somber glances at the growing mound of debris that is rising up around us as I continue to haul home my treasures from the hills, I say with pride and satisfaction: "I'm glad I've got rocks in my head!"

Epilogue

Toward a Better Squirrel Cage

Are you glad you escaped from the Squirrel Cage?

Do you secretly wish you could return to it?

These are the questions my friends ask me, and which privately I ask myself.

In trying to answer them I think back over the years since I became the wife of my horse lover.

It hasn't been an idle life.

At any hour of the day or night I'm apt to hear:

"Rubye! Hurry! Big Mama has a fox tail in her eye. Take those tweezers, while I hold her, and see if you can get it out."

I suck in my viscera to allow as much space as possible between Big Mama's huge forefoot and me, I stand on tiptoe, look Big Mama squarely in her brown, marbled eye—and extract the fox tail.

"Rubye! Come quick! Hold this twitch while I clip Lolly's ears. He won't stand still without it."

A twitch is a short piece of wood about the size and shape of a billy club with a loop at one end of it. The loop is twined about the prehensile end of a horse's nose and the handle twisted. The horse knows, as he feels the twitch tighten on his nose, that any movement will cause it to tighten more, so he stands still. Holding a twitch is a job I hate because it always hurts me more than it does the horse. But I have learned to do it.

217

"Rubye! Hurry! Patches has herself cast!"

This means Patches has hooked her legs under a fence and can't get free. One of us has to sit on her neck while the other slips a rope around her legs and carefuly pulls her around till she can be released. I always draw neck-sitting position since I can't pull hard enough to be any help at the other end.

"Rubye! Come pull this wood out of Dan's mouth while I hold his jaws open; he's wedged a stick between his teeth!"

I could do the job a lot faster if I wouldn't close my eyes. But every time I look in that big mouth with its king-size teeth my eyes automatically shut and I have to start over again. Eventually we extract the wood, but I'm not much good for anything by the time we finish.

"Ruby! Come hold this hose on this horse's leg while I feed. Keep it running till the swelling goes down."

Forty-five minutes later I remember I put a cake in the oven just befer THE CALL came!

"Frank! Frank!"

No answer. He's gone to the back pasture and I smell the cake burning.

"Aren't you glad you get a sit-down job once in a while?" asks Frank when he finally comes back.

Ranch life is rugged and ranch life is rough. Ranch life is dust and danger, mud and hard labor, and the ever-lasting counting of pennies to see if you can make them stretch. Ranch life is also mountains and stars and the mystery of birth and the wonder of growth and the sweetness of working with your husband—ranch life is a constant outpouring of love.

But if you were to ask me if I've really escaped from the Squirrel Cage, I'd have to ask you, does anyone? Or do we simply exchange one Squirrel Cage for a better one? I believe we do! I believe we always move toward a better Squirrel Cage; and as far as I'm concerned I've found mine. There isn't anything on earth I'd rather be than a ranch wife; and there's no place on earth I'd rather live than at the Bar None—in this valley in the hollow of God's hand.